DESIGN-
BUILD STUDIOS
IN LATIN AMERICA
Teaching Through
a Social Agenda

ORO Editions
Publishers of Architecture, Art, and Design
Gordon Goff: Publisher

www.oroeditions.com
info@oroeditions.com

Published by ORO Editions

Author:
Felipe Mesa, Ana Valderrama, and Gustavo Diéguez
Book Design:
Mesa estándar / Juan David Díez and Miguel Mesa
Project Manager:
Jake Anderson
Translator:
Fionn Petch
Copyediting Spanish texts:
Luisa Correa

10 9 8 7 6 5 4 3 2 1 First Edition

ISBN:
978-1-957183-38-1

Color Separations and Printing:
ORO Group Inc.

Printed in China

ORO Editions makes a continuous effort to minimize the
overall carbon footprint of its publications. As part of this
goal, ORO, in association with Global ReLeaf, arranges
to plant trees to replace those used in the manufacturing
of the paper produced for its books. Global ReLeaf is an
international campaign run by American Forests, one of
the world's oldest nonprofit conservation organizations.
Global ReLeaf is American Forests' education and action
program that helps individuals, organizations, agencies, and
corporations improve the local and global environment by
planting and caring for trees.

Graham Foundation

Design-Build Studios in Latin America

TEACHING THROUGH A SOCIAL AGENDA

ORO
EDITIONS

Con-
tents

Ac-knowl-edg-ments

Graham Foundation

This project received a 2022 publications grant from the **Graham Foundation for Advanced Studies in the Fine Arts**. We would like to express our gratitude for its support and commitment to the development and exchange of diverse and challenging ideas around architecture and its role in the arts, culture, and society. In particular, our thanks to Sarah Herda, Director; James Pike, Program Officer; and Carolyn Kelly, Grant Manager.

This project also received a HIRBI Fall Grant 2022 from the Herberger Research Council at the Herberger Institute for Design and the Arts, Arizona State University. We are grateful for this support; our particular thanks to Sandra L. Stauffer, Senior Associate Dean; Theo Eckhardt, Asst. Director of Research Advancement; and Shauna Allison, Business Operations Manager.

At ORO Editions and Applied Research + Design Publishers, we would like to thank Gordon Goff, Founder and Executive Publisher; and Jake Anderson, Chief Operating Officer, for their support and commitment to this project. At Mesaestándar, our thanks to Miguel Mesa and Juan David Díez, for their support and creative contributions to this book.

We would like to thank all the professors, architects, students, organizations, communities, and universities that participated in this project. Without their work, effort, and willingness to collaborate, the preparation and publication of this book would have been impossible.

Felipe Mesa would like to thank the team at Plan:b arquitectos, especially Federico Mesa and Laura Correa, for their unconditional support, providing the time and space necessary for the preparation of this book. Felipe would also like to thank several people at The Design School Architecture Program of the Herberger Institute for Design and The Arts at Arizona State University: Paola Sanguinetti, Director, The Design School; Marc Neveu, former Head, Architecture Program; Claudio Vekstein, Head, Architecture Graduate Program; Elena Rocci, Head, Architecture Undergraduate Program; and Professors Catherine Spellman, Darren Petrucci, and Renata Hejduk. Finally, Felipe Mesa thanks architect Andrés Jaque for his support.

Ana Valderrama would like to express her thanks to the Matéricos Periféricos team at the Universidad Nacional de Rosario, Argentina, and to the University of Illinois Urbana-Champaign, for providing spaces of joint construction, intellectual feedback, and daily practice.

Gustavo Diéguez would like to thank the Universidad Nacional de San Martín, Argentina, for the continued support of the Institute of Architecture and Urbanism.

The Quest for the Real

**FABRIZIO
GALLANTI**

Since time immemorial, architects have dealt with the difficulties of predicting the future, through design. In Romance languages, the term "design" is equivalent to the words *progetto*, *projet*, *proyecto*, from the Latin *projectus* meaning "to launch something forward," hence actively foreseeing the future.

A tangible and real object (a space—a building, to simplify) is executed after a complex sequence of actions has first been taken to imagine such an entity, then all the subsequent steps leading to its construction, and at the end, the actual act of building. The first two phases—imagining a building and laying out the sequence of activities bringing it to execution—constitute what conventionally is considered "design" or "project." Numerous scholars have identified in the Italian Renaissance, with the construction of the dome for the cathedral of Florence by Filippo Brunelleschi and the treatises of Leon Battista Alberti, the emergence of the modern figure of the architect as distinct from the builder. Through drawings and instructions, the architect thinks of construction in abstract terms and then coordinates others to execute it under his guidance. Over centuries, the tension between the intellectual act of imagining a building and the technicalities of actually "making" it has been at the core of architecture. Architects were learning their trade by working in the ateliers of older mentors or, later, studying at the fine arts academies. It was only because of industrialization and the appearance of a new professional figure, the engineer, that architecture schools emerged at the end of the nineteenth century in Europe and the U.S. Even today, their teaching methodologies bridge these two lineages. On the one hand, around representation, stemming from the Beaux-Arts heritage (think of the "charrette"). On the other hand, around construction, imbued with the legacy of civil engineering (think of calculus, still a trying obstacle for first-year students).

Since the affirmation of Bauhaus-inspired educational protocols in the first half of the twentieth century, a doubt has continued to trouble many of those involved in architectural teaching: is it possible to learn how to build only in the abstract and only by drawing? Once on the construction site, will freshly graduated architects know how "things" actually work just because they have studied, redrawn, and invented technical details at the 1:5 or 1:1 scale? How will they be able to sit down at the table with engineers and contractors?

In response to such doubts, the conviction that the act of building can be apprehended only by doing has led a growing number of architecture schools worldwide to execute 1:1 projects built by students and incorporated within their curricula. The construction site, conventionally placed at the end of the methodology of architectural design, has returned to the core of learning, even if it is at the size of a pavilion, a small house, the arrangement of a defined public space. Around it, all the different fields of expertise converge, the materials—with their weight and texture—are mobilized, and physical labor is engaged. Moreover, the phantasmal figure of the "user" appears, as all these projects have one or several: in the most basic versions, the students and faculty themselves; in other more ambitious endeavors, real communities and inhabitants, with their desires and needs.

Such an approach, first seen in numerous Bauhaus-inspired schools, and continued through the experimentations of alternative institutions such as the Black Mountain College or the Pontifical Catholic University in Valparaíso in the 1960s and '70s, has established itself across very diverse contexts. Rural Studio at Auburn University in Alabama, the ALICE laboratory at the EPFL in Lausanne, and the Solar Decathlon competition are just a few examples of this growing interest.

In the Latin American context, precursors such as the design-build studio Travesías at the Pontifical Catholic University in Valparaíso or the graduation thesis projects at Talca University, both in Chile, have inspired numerous initiatives that are the subject of this publication. Three general features are identified across all the case studies in the book: the proximity to craft and working methods, still far from the highly industrialized and prefabricated systems found in the U.S. or northern Europe; the attention to an urban condition where vast portions of the urban realm are informal and self-built; and the intention to provide valuable solutions, in close exchange with local communities. The projects become real not only because they are built and occupy a tangible presence but because they are imbued with the necessities and expectations of future users: they are rarely academic and formal exercises but rather tactical responses that increase people's quality of life. They generate novel, hybrid forms of architectural thinking, where the feedback loops in the exchange with the users and during the construction process alter in deep and meaningful ways the linearity of the conventional design process, inherited from the modernist mythology. This approach is essentially "learning by doing," where learning is not limited to academic years but instead becomes a permanent approach applied to each future project, and remains present well into the professional career.

These design-build studios suggest the emergence of a new and different model for the architect; perhaps as a more practical intellectual, who is deeply engaged in the processes of transformation rather than directing them from above. An architect knowledgeable about construction and open to incorporating the skills of others into more horizontal systems of knowledge and power. We can also say that—perhaps unconsciously—this quest for the "real" pursues an ambitious and romantic objective of rolling back time, returning to an idealized moment, perhaps in the Middle Ages, when there were no architects as we know them today, but master builders.

Con- straints and Agree- ments

FELIPE MESA

This publication presents the work of fourteen design-build studios from across Latin America: Mexico, Colombia, Venezuela, Ecuador, Paraguay, Chile, Argentina, and Uruguay. It assembles thirty-nine small-format constructions with social programs—classrooms, pavilions, platforms, refuges, community centers, libraries, cafeterias, stages, dry toilets, pergolas—on which professors, students, community leaders, municipal representatives, nongovernmental organizations, and private companies worked together. Today, these spaces are maintained and used by communities of students, farmers, local residents, fishers, female heads of household, or sportspeople. Drawing on the case studies, this book makes clear the complexity involved in the design-build process in partnership with communities, rejecting the notion that it is a purely formal matter.

The investigation considers the various constraints in play—whether inherent, imposed, or self-imposed—as elements beneficial to the discipline that serve to generate positive and unexpected situations, rather than as external limitations on creative freedom. It employs concrete examples to reinforce the idea that good buildings need not necessarily be large, long-lasting, unique, expensive, imposing, or high-tech. To the contrary, it showcases small, ephemeral, ordinary, low-cost, and subtle constructions that use mixed technology to have a positive impact on their communities. It proposes that a quality education in architecture does not have to be individual, elitist, isolated, and competitive, but can be socially committed, connected to its context, and collaborative. In this sense, *Design-Build Studios in Latin America: Teaching through a Social Agenda* not only puts forward necessary positions and urgent strategies for education and the contemporary practice of architecture, but also offers new tools to bring our discipline closer to society and its growing problems, without abandoning the considered search for innovative aesthetic qualities.

The partially bilingual book (English and Spanish), aimed at an audience of students, architects, designers, artists, activists, government agencies, and a wider public interested in material practices and social commitment, is the first publication to cover the leading design-build studios in Latin America, with their social agendas and collaborative projects.

In the Latin American context, this compilation brings together work carried out over the past two decades, reviewing points of similarity, differences, and future opportunities. For the rest of the world, the project, with its emphasis on limitations as a positive phenomenon, aims to expand our knowledge of design-build studios.

In the academic sphere, the book hopes to encourage the creation of new studios that boost the teaching of architecture with social agendas and the construction of buildings or spaces with tangible benefits for the communities that use them. In the professional context, it offers a set of values, qualities, and projects that seek to shake up architects' way of thinking and daily practices. In the field of independent and government organizations, the book presents a catalog of options and strategies for promoting new projects for the benefit of students and specific communities.

Although the fourteen case studies we present here involve a range of different kinds of alliances with municipal governments, NGOs, private enterprise, or communities, broadly speaking the book covers two principal types of design-build studios. On one hand, those that form a central and long-term part of a university curriculum: Travesías Studio, Talca Graduation Studio, Matéricos Periféricos Studio, PAAF Studio, Danza Studio, E Studio, Intervención Comunitaria Studio, and PEI Studio. On the other hand, those that formed a temporary part of an academic structure, but have since disappeared or adapted to institutional changes in search of greater stability: Nubes de Madera Studio, Lab.Pro.Fab Studio, Al Borde Studio, Atarraya Studio, a77 Studio, and Activo Studio. A number of cases, such as a77, Al Borde, or Lab.Pro.Fab, emerged and remain as professional practices closely connected with social work and architecture education through established courses in a number of universities.

In all the case studies presented here, the architectural design was prepared by a group of professors and students in partnership with communities and technical advisors. There are three different modes of construction. In the first, certain studios have institutional conditions for their students to build with their own hands (with a range of insurance methods and liabilities), leaving only a few of the processes to experts. In the second, partnerships are established with construction companies that take on the legal responsibilities, enabling students to form part of a construction team led by experts. Finally, the third modality comprises courses that hand over most of the responsibility for the construction to partner companies and experts who take on the civil responsibility, with the students focusing on works supervision and smaller construction processes carried out in the university shops.

In most cases, the entire planning, design, and build process takes an academic semester and involves a similar working schedule: one month for general outlines; two months for design, details, securing resources and permissions; and one month to build. In some cases the times are longer, with the courses using one or two semesters for planning and design, and one for construction. Some courses are designed for first-year students—it is important to clarify that to graduate with a degree in architecture in Latin America requires five years, or ten academic semesters—putting them in immediate contact with communities, materials, and construction processes. Others accept students in third and fourth years, and foster interaction with different experiences in order to face the challenges of the process. Finally, a number of universities leave these courses for the final year and allow students greater independence in how they address them. In almost all cases, however, students are building their first project before graduating.

What is unique about design-build studios in Latin America is the effort they make to simultaneously generate quality education and real impacts in communities that are marginalized or have specific needs. To do this without ceding the interest in different aspects of the discipline, professors and students together design participation strategies—meetings, conversations, journeys, crossings, visits, roundtables, participatory workshops, interviews, surveys—to define locations, programs, materials, construction systems, and future maintenance. They also expend a great deal of energy on seeking financial resources, for which they implement a wide range of mixed strategies: institutional support from universities, raffles, student events, support from family members, municipal governments and private companies, grants, local or foreign donations, and online fundraising. Sometimes professors suggest that students reduce to a minimum the production of representations (models and printed materials) in order to channel the available funds to the final construction. No course is identical to any other, but all blend to a different degree the same elements that make it possible to build in a very short time small-format interventions in which the restrictions and agreements shape the architecture.

The Valparaíso Design-Build Studio[2]—identified in this book as the Travesías Studio—is the only such studio to have emerged in the mid-twentieth century. Due to its tradition and its emphasis on the journey, as well as travel and provisional and poetic interventions in the rural landscape, it had a major influence on all other design-build studios in Latin America, whether directly or indirectly. The current interest in this type of studio in Latin America reflects a renewed focus on teaching architecture in a manner that is closer to people, materials, and construction processes, as well as the political changes that occurred at the end of the twentieth and early twenty-first centuries, when countries like Argentina, Brazil, Uruguay, Venezuela, Colombia, and Chile, which were led by neoliberal governments, made way for social democrat administrations with a greater concern for reducing the region's endemic inequality. The response to these political and educational situations takes on different nuances in each of the cases presented here: in general terms, some develop ties with urban communities, build small-format public facili-

ties, and activate underused spaces (Matéricos Periféricos Studio, a77 Studio, Danza Studio, E Studio, Lab.Pro.Fab Studio, Intervención Comunitaria Studio, Activo Studio). Others, in partnership with rural communities, engage in small-format interventions with both ecological and social benefits (Nubes de Madera Studio, Talca Graduation Studio, Al Borde Studio, PAAF Studio, PEI Studio, Atarraya Studio, Travesías Studio).

Publications by a number of the studios examined here lay out their academic underpinnings more fully. The School of Architecture and Design of the Pontifical Catholic University, Valparaíso, Chile, published the book *Amereida*;[3] the School of Architecture of Talca, Chile, published the book *Talca, cuestión de educación*;[4] the Matéricos Periféricos Studio of the Universidad de Rosario, Argentina, published the book *Poéticas colectivas*;[5] the Nubes de Madera Studio at the Faculty of Architecture of the Pontifical Bolivarian University, Colombia, published the book *Nubes de madera*;[6] and the Language and Creation Hub of the Faculty of Architecture, Design, and Construction of the UDLA, Chile, and its Community Intervention Studio published the book *Academia como práctica*.[7]

Although these Latin American studios have developed in an independent and isolated fashion, it is important to mention a number of global reference points that have been of clear relevance. The most influential case for the Latin American context may be the Rural Studio[8] at Auburn University in the United States, whose sustained work over the past three decades has been widely disseminated. This design-build studio, founded in 1993 by Samuel Mockbee (1944–2001) and D. K. Ruth (1944–2009), and today directed by Andrew Freear, places the emphasis on teaching architecture students through the design and construction of small-format buildings and interventions—housing, infrastructure, and public spaces—with a significant and positive impact on the daily lives of rural and vulnerable communities in Hale County, Alabama.

It is also important to emphasize that in the context of the United States and Europe there is an established tradition of design-build studios, as made clear by two recent publications. Firstly, the book *The Design-Build Studio: Crafting Meaningful Work in Architecture Education*,[9] edited by Tolya Stonorov and published in 2018, brings together articles and case studies from U.S. and European universities. Secondly, the book *Experience in Action: DesignBuild in Architecture*,[10] edited by Vera Simone Bader and Andres Lepik, and published as part of an exhibition of the same name, compiles articles, essays, interviews, and sixteen case studies from Europe, the U.S., and around the world. In this latter publication, although all the universities are from the U.S. and Europe—with the exception of the Universidad de Morón, in Argentina—in a number of cases they worked in countries in the southern hemisphere, such as Cambodia, Argentina, India, South Africa, and Cameroon. Both publications develop work in parallel to that presented in this book, and reflect the growing interest in this educational and participatory model in the global context.

Generally speaking, we can say that design-build studios in the U.S., in Europe, and in Latin America all share similar characteristics, though the first two explore with greater intensity certain technical innovations—construction methods, materials, 3D printing, to name a few—and the latter focus more on social innovations such as participation methods, listening and inclusion strategies, and management of financial resources, among others, always determined by highly restrictive contexts that make necessary the use of local or mixed construction techniques.

This book is structured into independent chapters, enabling comparison and cross-referencing of information between case studies, but it can also be read as a whole, bringing together the diversity of this labor into a single collective effort. It opens with three essays that explore the theme from different angles: the political role of these studios, what the world can learn from them, and one of their principal strategies—listening. These are followed by the fourteen case studies with their academic and social approaches, key projects from each, and a collection of images of their processes. Finally, the book closes with a commentary focused on the pedagogical and disciplinary qualities of this architecture, in which the social emphasis defines specific tectonic qualities.

1. Jon Elster, *Ulysses Unbound* (Cambridge: Cambridge University Press, 2000), 190-221.
2. Beatriz Colomina et al., eds., *Radical Pedagogies* (Cambridge, MA: MIT Press, 2022), 154-59.
3. *Amereida: travesías 1984 a 1988* (Valparaíso: Ediciones e[ad], 2011).
4. José Luis Uribe Ortiz, ed., *Talca, cuestión de educación* (Mexico D.F.: Arquine, 2013).
5. Ana Valderrama et al., *Poéticas colectivas* (Buenos Aires: Bisman Ediciones, 2018).
6. Felipe Mesa and Miguel Mesa, *Nubes de madera* (Medellín: Mesaestándar, 2017).
7. Fernando Portal, ed., *Academia como práctica* (Santiago de Chile: Ediciones Academia Espacial, 2020).
8. Andrew Freear et al., *Rural Studio at Twenty: Designing and Building in Hale County, Alabama* (New York: Princeton Architectural Press, 2014).
9. Tolya Stonorov, ed., *Design-Build Studio: Crafting Meaningful Work in Architecture Education* (New York: Routledge, 2018).
10. Vera Simone Bader and Andres Lepik, eds., *Experience in Action: DesignBuild in Architecture* (Munich: DETAIL, 2020).

Design-Build Studios. Entanglements and Decoloniality

ANA VALDERRAMA

When our lived experience of theorizing is fundamentally linked to processes of self-recovery, of collective liberation, no gap exists between theory and practice.

In this essay I want to contribute to the debate on the decolonial theories and practices of the Global South by exploring correlations between the processes and products of design-build studios and the socio-political dynamics in which they are entangled. Design-build studios may be understood as belonging to the many experiences of situated or land-based teaching practices developed in the context of decolonial methodologies. Feminist, indigenous, queer, and other methodologies have made and continue to make a great contribution to resisting dispossession processes by deploying in situ, in vivo experiences that reconnect the body with the land, understanding land and bodies as the principal territories of dispute for capitalism today. Understanding the land as an integral entity that includes plants, waters, humans, and non-humans, these methodologies propose integrated, situated, collective, and dialogical practices capable of articulating diverse forms of knowledge and inters-transcor-intra-agencies.

I am interested in exhibiting the potential of design-build studios beyond their standard teaching agendas. That is, in light of their capacity for countering processes of becoming inoculated against mechanisms of alienation and dispossession, and for breaking down modern dichotomies that prevent the understanding of complex phenomena. Inevitably my position is that of a Latin American woman, activist, and co-founder of the architects' collective Matéricos Periféricos, based in Rosario, Argentina.

Matéricos Periféricos emerged during the Argentine financial and institutional crisis of 2001, and constituted an activist group of university professors, design professionals, and students, dedicated to building facilities and infrastructure with communities experiencing social and environmental emergencies, through design-build studios. The studios function as mechanisms to strengthen social life within vulnerable communities and to support grassroots and neighborhood organizations in their resistance to the mechanisms of real power.

This essay offers an epistemological and ontological reflection, one that is as much about the political cultural position and direction of our practices in relation to the discipline, taking the central role of the periphery, as it is about the being of artifacts, their processes of materialization, and their form as the expression of a resistance to the processes of dispossession that occur in these peripheries. Those practices need to be re-explored and theorized since public policies and literature about design—at all scales—"for" the dispossessed have frequently followed the prescriptions of the global colonizing political and disciplinary apparatus to penetrate communities and deactivate resistance. That is to say, their reflections and actions are based on the fetishization and commercialization of the tools of resistance, converting them into patronage or charity—leading to idealized, packaged solutions that have failed to take local community, materials, energy flow, and cultures into account—or based on a romanticized and/or conformist notion of informality that reproduces the forms and expressions of poverty, preventing other dreams from emerging. In this regard, the review of our practices rooted in certain theoretical speculations about the socio-material world could allow us to figure ideas previously unimagined and thereby interpret, challenge, and confer new meanings to our works. Ultimately, as bell hooks suggests, theoretical speculation is an emancipatory practice as well.[3]

HOUSE TAKEN OVER

> The consciousness of the world, which makes my consciousness possible, makes impossible the immutability of the world.[4]

Peripheries of the Global South are the territories in which capitalist mechanisms for fulfilling "accumulation by dispossession"[5] are exposed obscenely at the extreme of the spectacle, materializing all of Debord's ironies. Cecilia Chu and Romola Sanyal[6] state that the proclamation of Guy Debord in 1967 about the spectacle as a principle of modern societies has triumphed in recent decades with neoliberal capitalist globalization and the commodification of the built environment. Unrepresented communities in the Global South have been, in fact, a constant variable for the survival of capitalism. That is, the systematic expulsion of the poor towards the peripheries has generated a cheap labor force and easy accumulation of capital, while people are pushed further and further towards marginal fields, inhospitable lands, places without infrastructure, flood zones, undeveloped sites. After the Second World War, this process of displacement, stigmatization, and dispossession accelerated with the help of international credit bodies, global decentralization, division of labor (race, gender, class, space, time), and the separation between global economic power and local political administration. From then to the present day, capitalism's metamorphic ability has commodified everything it could find in its path (even solidarity initiatives, participatory strategies, NGOs), and the socio-spatial meshwork of cities has been the main platform for capital flow, generating deeper social instability and inequity.

Nowadays, the forces of capitalism are totally detached from geography, law, institutions, and governments, and are characterized by greedy, speculative processes that take the form of the depletion of nature and the systematic construction of social, economic, and ecological instability, inequity, and injustice. During this process, city planners have completely lost sight of the original goal of reducing the gap between the rich and the poor to the right to the city, as modern urbanism proclaimed in the twentieth century. On the contrary, planning has become just a tool to legitimize real-estate speculation and international organisms' prescriptions to demobilize and weaken insurgent practices. In most cases, professionals have been ornaments to give prestige to local officials' clientelism and charity, or have published politically correct plans that will never materialize. Peripheries of the Global South are like Julio Cortázar's short story "House Taken Over,"[7] in which an omnipresent but invisible entity forces the characters to retreat and move backwards from one room to the other. At the end of the tale, the characters escape from the house and throw the keys into a sewer. Can we change the end of the tale?

CORRELATION OF FORCES

> When there are stars, there are eels born in the Atlantic depths that begin, because we have to begin to follow them, … mouths that slide in an interminable suction … will rise up leviathan, emerge as an inoffensive and terrifying kraken, to initiate the migration along the ocean floor.[8]

Collective practices of decolonial design move always between the gaps and overlaps of hierarchical (top-bottom) and self-organized or meshwork (bottom-up and to the side) processes that interact and change over time, giving rise to processes of formation and transformation of built environments. Hierarchies and meshworks coexist, intermingle, and give rise to one another. Manuel DeLanda[9] understands these processes of formation and transformation in an ontological manner. According to him, cities arise from self-organized processes of flow of matter and energy, but when they stabilize in a form, hierarchical forces react to create new constraints that intensify or prevent their growth through the forces of homogenization and centralization.

That is, urban environments start by emerging from an ecology of institutions (schools, universities, markets) that take collective decisions. However, once they are stable, they are centralized by government bureaucracy, which uses those structures to dominate and homogenize the society that gave shape to them. Deleuze and Guattari,[10] for their part, understand the dynamics between hierarchical and self-organized forces as a double articulation, like the coexisting pincers of a lobster. They illustrate this concept through the *machine of faces*. A *machine of faces* has two facets: *white walls* and *black holes*. *White walls* represent the colonizing production of the face, capitalism, hierarchical forces, strata, striated space, and lines of segmentation (that codify and territorialize). *Black holes* represent the social production of face, insurgency, the *war machines*, self-organized forces, the *Body without Organs*, the smooth space and the lines of flight (that de-code and de-territorialize to produce becoming).

INSURGENCY

> Nezahualcoyotl one day said:
> The two main courses of university education:
> Ixlamachiliztli [give wisdom to faces]
> Yolmelahualiztli [straighten hearts]
> …
> The Ministry of Poetry
> Open all day. The one of war
> almost always closed.[11]

Collective practices of decolonial design attempt to counter an alternative project on the basis of active participation in the correlations of force that enter the cracks of the totalizing, hegemonic, and unequal project of the cities. Cecilia L. Chu and Romola Sanyal state that

> capitalism can never be reduced to pure logics of capital accumulation, and that the modern metropolis is not only an arena of domination but also of contestation and political struggles that always carries the potentials for revolutionary change.[12]

Richard Falks,[13] for his part, proposes a movement of resistance that he calls *globalization from below*, that consists of strengthening local identities. Manfred Max-Neef[14] also highlights the value of defending and protecting identities as a mode of resistance. He describes the values and principles of unrepresented communities in Chile that arose from the ashes of capitalism and resisted the culture of greed: solidarity, creativity, networks of cooperation, mutual aid. Seo Bongman,[15] is much more pessimistic: for him, the globalized system has systematically increased poverty, destruction of national industries, and the instability of finances though international debt with the phantom of so-called "development," and he discards any possibility of reconciliation between the Global South and the globalized system. Between the optimism of resistance and the pessimism of the impossibility of reconciliation, what are the possibilities, the modes of operating of the practices of decolonial design in the Global South? In "Insurgent Practices and Decolonization of Future(s)," Faranak Miraftab[16] proposes insurgency as a way out, and defines two kinds of insurgent spaces: invited and inventing. Invited spaces are defined by grassroots actions through community-based informal groups in alliance with governments and other institutions. Inventing spaces are collective actions by the poor that directly confront the authorities and challenge and destabilize the status quo. Insurgent practices defined by Miraftab move across both invited and inventing spaces, since they need to be fluid and move faster than capitalism. Their actions are sometimes pacific, sometimes violent, both outside and inside the established law. They are actions that address transgression, counter hegemony, and engage the imagination to make another, radically different world emerge.

FRAGMENTS, CO-EXISTENCES, MULTIPLICITIES

> The collage is thus the most appropriate technique to manifest the seething disparity of our realities: the coexistence of flagrant inequalities, contemporary antagonisms, explosive contrasts. The collage is the combination that makes it possible to actively symbolize the mobile and heterogeneous multiplicity of reality.[17]

Two fundamental questions therefore present themselves: How could our design-build studios, in their processes and materializations, predict an emerging aesthetics of society and play a role in a project of emancipation both of society and of the discipline? What would the strategy of the design-build studios be in order to penetrate the cracks of the hegemonic project? Walter Benjamin would say "for the first time in world history, technological reproducibility emancipates the work of art from its parasitic subservience to ritual … Instead of being founded on ritual, it is based on a different practice: politics."[18]

Walter Benjamin stated that the emergence of the means of technical production and reproduction had produced a de-sacralization of art or put in crisis the aura of art.[19] This was similar to what Adorno called the "crisis of aesthetic appearance of totality,"[20] although for him this was not a product of the means of technical reproduction but a response to the historical conditions of reality, which he considered contradictory and no longer accessible to our rationality. Benjamin was interested in exploring the intersection between art, revolution, the modes of production—in particular, the reproduction of artworks and the art of film—and human sensory and cognitive processes. Revolutionary art for him was one capable of finding fractures in the system from where it could provoke the rupture of the dominant culture's sense of continuity through constellations. Constellations could put forward alternative worlds able to increase the correlations of forces. Benjamin saw films as an example of how figures of thought or dialectical images could generate otherwise inaccessible or unrepresentable meanings. Films were montages of fragments or constellations that provoked a reaction and gave access to new possible worlds.[21] The camera introduced a dialectical movement of distraction-shock that turned the work of art into a weapon as well as a "training" for the viewer to learn to look at reality in other ways. "Film has freed the physical shock effect—which Dadaism had kept wrapped, as it were, inside the moral shock effect—from this wrapping."[22]

Later, in 1980, Gilles Deleuze and Félix Guattari[23] offered an alternative to the totality of capitalism through schizophrenia,[24] and proposed the "rhizome" as a model, both to provide a means of confronting the dominant hegemonic cultures, as well as to operate in the socio-material world. The rhizome was a multiplicity that emerged from non-hierarchical, self-organizing processes. It was a heterogeneous arrangement that confronted Hegelian totalities and arborescent conceptions. Their *agencements*[25] were conceived as multiplicities of agencies or connections and relationships of contents and expressions within a socio-material world. These *agencements* could take the form of *strata*, *assemblages*, or *bodies without organs*, depending on the intensity of territorialization and the codification of components. Manuel DeLanda later synthetized the ontology of *assemblage* as a multiplicity that

> has proprieties on its own, not reducible to the parts that also maintain their autonomy. Parts exercise certain capacities when they interact with one another, but they could be detached from the assemblage at any time. The identity of the assemblage at any point in space and time will be determined by a set of parameters and intensities of territorialization and codification.[26]

REHEARSALS INSTEAD OF SPECTACLES

> Poetry must be done by everybody. And not for oneself. … Poetry in action emerges and inserts itself into reality. It reveals the possibility that all effective existence founds and at the same time becomes an act in the world. I have then seen the poet leaving literature, surpassing the poem, and even abandoning writing.[27]

Theodor Adorno and Walter Benjamin stated that after Auschwitz, the world had lost all traces of humanity and had become incomprehensible to our eyes. They asked themselves what the purpose of art is in this unfathomable and inhuman world, how art could express this inhuman reality in its form, its image, its materiality, its production processes. Benjamin was interested in the potential of cinema as a form of resistance, above all in the way this discipline promoted participatory processes and appropriated current means of production. Benjamin understood film as a performance produced and reproduced through a participatory project mediated by technology. In his view, the spectator is incorporated into the production process by participating in it through the standpoint of the camera eye. In this way, the spectator is also a critic and completes the work of art.[28]

Benjamin thought of the artwork as a weapon or as "training" for the spectator to learn to look at reality in other ways. Theodor Adorno, meanwhile, thought that art wasn't meant to change the world, but to change itself in order to express and portray the incomprehensibility of the world. There was no direct relationship for him between the reflection of art and the praxis of revolution. In this sense, Adorno was interested in the Theater of the Absurd of Beckett and Ionesco, among others. This theater of the absurd was the theater that expressed the meaninglessness of the world by dismantling the discipline from within, deconstructing the meaning of dialogue, the relationships between message and words, habitual procedures, the pretension to final form taken by the theater scene. From the Latin American perspective, Augusto Boal made a similar contribution by gathering the experiences of the Theater of Sand and Freire's formulations. Yet Boal thought that art could in fact be a mechanism of social transformation, that there was a relationship between art and revolution, and wrote a book called *Poetic Politics*,[29] later known as *Theater of the Oppressed*.[30] Unlike Benjamin's films, in Boal's *Theater of the Oppressed* the spectator does not delegate to the professional actor the power to think or to act in their place. Spectators take on responsibility for the performance, dismantle the structure of their own bodies and minds, alter the theatrical action, try out solutions, and debate evolutions of the scene. That is, they train in the actual theatrical action. In this case, it could be that theater is not revolutionary in itself, but is a training for revolution. Theater was a movement from reality towards ideality (and not the other way around), and the seed for revolutionary change. Augusto Boal said that theater should tear down the walls imposed by the dominant classes: everybody should perform, everybody should actively engage in the transformations. Boal called it a "wildcard system" that meant "the conquest of the means of theatrical production"[31] by the oppressed. Therefore, the role of theater is to activate our awareness of our own reality, of the structural forces of oppression, and to imagine strategies for emancipation. Boal's theater is a theater-rehearsal, not a theater-spectacle. It is the theater of process, without preconceived form. In *Theater of the Oppressed*, rather than a closed script, there is a kind of flexible infrastructure that allows for improvisations, additions, and omissions. So, it is always unfinished, and people can continue adding or taking things away. Finally, the value of *Theater of the Oppressed* resides in the process, not the product.

COAGULATIONS

> I am interested in getting to Time in its unstructured existence. That is, I am interested in how this wild beast lives in the jungle—not in the zoo. I am interested in how Time exists before we put our paws on it—our minds, our imagination into it.[32]

The artifacts built by design-build studios cannot be understood from the Albertian form of the discipline, that is, as a process that moves from the preconceived image of a form to its construction. These artifacts are, instead, coagulated moments—of forces, energies, and matter—that emerge as the result of a multiple and dialogic meshwork of human and non-human wills over time. This presupposes a paradigm shift in the conception of the material world. In *On the Nature of the Universe*,[33] Roman poet and philosopher Lucretius conceives the world as a continuity of matter-energy in which everything (humans and non-humans) is composed of the same infinite substance and in which all possibilities are available:

> I will reveal those atoms from which nature creates all things. ... To these in my discourse I commonly give such names as the *raw material*, or generative bodies or *seeds of things*. Or I may

call them *primary particles,* because they come first and everything else is composed of them.[34]

In this continuum world, matter-energies have creative capacities that are expressed in their immanent ability to self-organize
and acquire different forms. But how do these matter-energies
self-organize into things? Jane Bennett[35] suggests that there is
a constantly forming and reforming process of materialization
by virtue of an intrinsic *vitality.* In other words, matter-energies
have their own vitality that allow them to self-organize into
things that also have their own agency and intended motion with
directionality and causality.[36] Manuel DeLanda,[37] for his part,
claims that it is a flow that allows matter-energy to self-organize
and acquire contingent shape. Dynamic flows of matter-energy
and information with semi-stable qualities and different expressions (geological, biological, and linguistic) pass through human
and non-human bodies and populations and became mineral-
ized, giving form to things in the material world. Gilles Deleuze
and Félix Guattari develop the concept of *agencements*[38] to
explore the capacity of matter-energy to form structures at
macro scales.

An *agencement* is a multiplicity of inter-agencies of heterogeneous components (tangible or intangible materials and expressions) that interact and flow, giving shape to assemblages,
strata, or bodies without organs.[39] But what makes these components remain attached to the *agencement*? Bennett tracks
this question in Spinoza, Serres, and Deleuze and Guattari.
According to her, Spinoza saw a tendency of matter to move and
give birth to forms or things when it is affected by the agency
of something else.[40] On the other hand, she states that Michael
Serres explains this tendency as the capacity of matter to "col-
lide, congeal, morph, evolve, and disintegrate by the action of
physics."[41] Finally, Bennett highlights Deleuze and Guattari's
concept of "nomadism of matter, or matter-movement, or matter in variation"[42] that enters and leaves the *agencements* due to
their nomadism, as well as due to their multiple interactions with
other entities and forces with different rates of speed and pace
of change.[43]

THE AGENCY OF ARTIFACTS

No one, of course, would occupy himself with such studies if there
were not a creature called Odradek.[44]

The complexity of the meshwork of forces that encompass
design-build studios, together with the material manifestations
of the artifacts after their materialization, require an inter-
agency analysis that the forms of production of architecture
had not foreseen. In his Actor Network Theory (ANT), Bruno

Latour[45] offers a semiotic approach to social interactions in which the social is rendered as a type of connection between humans and non-human *actants* (actors without figuration) in a framework of distributive *agencies*. In this regard, non-humans could play as active a role in the socio-material world as human beings. The author proposes a new branch of sociology called *sociology of associations*, as opposed to the traditional stable and fixed field of *sociology of the social* that has forgotten or ignored the existence of non-human entities, and has imposed pre-figurations on social aggregates and *inter-agentivities*. Jane Bennett[46] states that manmade items or "not-quite-things" have their own agency or a special force of independence.[47] They are actants with an active role in society since they have the capacity to relate or even alter humans and non-human bodies. Bennett describes the agency of things as *thing-power,* and provides specific examples to demonstrate that non-human materials as actants have an active role in society. She analyzes the metamorphic capacities of debris, the ability of inorganic matter to form entities and assemblages, the agency of legal actants (samples, material evidence, and deodans) as "something that acts or to which activity is granted by others," or as a "quasi-causal operator."[48] Bennett is also interested in understanding the distributed agency and the exponential power of assemblages when heterogeneous parts join and interact.[49] She appeals to Spinoza's concept of "conative bodies," in which bodies augment their power by associating with others[50] in a complex *mosaicized* arrangement. From Deleuze and Guattari, Bennett borrows the term "affective bodies," in the sense that there is a vitality in the multiplicity that augments when entities enter into collaboration, cooperation, or interactivity with other bodies and forces. In order to illustrate how agency works within assemblages, Bennett offers the example of an electrical power grid in a blackout event. In that event, some generators that are initially not connected to the assemblage provoke a change in patterns of electron flow that end up with an unexpected concatenation of episodes beyond the will, expectations, and imagination of humans, and at the same time, force other actants to connect to the assemblage.[51] Bennett calls it the *shi* of a vibratory assemblage.

ANCHORAGES

> The visible form of animals is, in effect, nothing more than a disguise. When they return to their homes, they do so to shed their appearance, covering themselves with feather ornaments and ceremonial ornaments ...[52]

The architectures and infrastructures co-constructed in design-build studios do not attempt to impose a form on matter in order to obtain an object. Rather, they attempt to combine materials and redirect their matter-energy flow in anticipation of what might emerge during the correlations of force involved in the co-construction process. Following this line of thought, we should think of the works as events that solidify as a result of the experience of the encounter between bodies and the material-natural world. Tim Ingold would say that "the process of genesis and growth that gives rise to the forms in the world we inhabit is more important than the form."[53] In "Materials against materiality," Tim Ingold[54] states that the world is a kind of sea of matter-energies that are in constant flux and correlation of forces. According to Ingold, human and non-human beings are meant to be immersed in and experience that material ocean through practical experience.[55] In "The textility of making,"[56] Ingold goes deeper into the idea of practical experience and asserts that the process of making is a performance in which we follow the flows of matter with our bodies through movements that are "itinerant, improvisatory and rhythmic."[57] Later, in *Being Alive*,[58] Ingold posits that that sea of matter-energies coagulates into threads when it is intercepted by living entities. Those threads are the traces of life along which processes of living, growing, or making take place, like a spider and its web. Once solidified, those traces cannot be detached from their environment, the currents, forces, and pressures that surround them. Like a kite in the air. "Cut out from these currents—that is, reduced to objects—they would be dead."[59] However, history has demonstrated that a design could be site-specific, and yet its matter-energies could have traveled across previous artifacts and be detached from them at any time to move to another place in the future as well. Enric Miralles said that architecture and things are not always in their place and that our memories travel from one place to another.[60] Similarly, Henri Focillon would argue that forms have a life of their own and travel from one entity to another even when they have different genetic origins.[61] That is, there exists a medium, but it does not determine totally the identity of entities because, in part, there is always our subjectivity. But, in addition, entities have an identity, an inner code that conditions the medium and the way they relate to it. As Deleuze and Guattari said, there are processes of de-territorialization and de-codification in which entities lose part of their inner code in order to be able to move—re-territorialize—from one environment to another.[62]

According to Deleuze and Guattari, the degree of codification and territorialization depends on the differentials of intensities and the correlation of forces between lines of segmentation and lines of flight that bend what they call the *Plane of Consistency.* We could say that the Plane of Consistency has the same metaphysical spirit as Lucretius's and Ingold's first stage of the world. Deleuze and Guattari say that their Plane of Consistency is omnipresent and traced by an *Abstract Machine* that operates in an original state characterized by a virtual continuum of matter-energy that initially contained all possibilities.[63] However, this Plane of Consistency could be transformed by the *war machines* that catalyze flows to create the conditions for transformation.[64] That is, the movements of matter-energy are processes of territorialization/de-territorialization, codification/de-codification that are deployed by the *war machines* through lines of segmentation and flight.[65] Deleuze and Guattari relate *war machines* with insurgents and nomad movements, who, while living and translating across the territory, propitiate the interruption and reverberation of changes of those omnipresent initial conditions.

DISCUSSIONS

Sordidness, from the series *The Cosmic Monsters,* 1964. Multi-media construction made of wood (general framework and smooth and pointed pieces), metals (steel, iron, bicycle brakes, antique flash projectors, header finials and soda caps), cardboard, plastic, dry shrub roots, nails and enamel. Platform included: 129 × 120 × 400 cm.[66]

The present conditions in the Global South, and in Argentina in particular, destabilize the fixed and direct correlations enunciated by Deleuze and Guattari with regard to governmental bureaucracy and hierarchical forces, representations of white walls and black holes, lines of flight and lines of segmentation. We could say that since the hierarchical forces of real power are highly fluid, invisible, and operate to de-stabilize, de-territorialize, and de-codify, insurgency should act in the opposite direction. Nowadays, real power is detached from the states, institutions, governments, political parties, and territories, and moves fluently to drain the world. After sucking the world far enough, it vanishes into thin air or hides in tax havens. During progressive governments, institutions are stabilized by self-organizing movements, and hierarchical forces work by injecting flows to de-territorialize and de-codify. In this respect, capitalism and insurgency could operate alternatively with the forms and actions of the other and use the entire range of existing possibilities to operate in the correlations of forces. The relationships between means and ends, strategies and tactics, ideologies and politics, are highly complex and contradictory nowadays. Hegemonic alienation and oppressive montages cannot be exposed, fractured, and disassembled all at once as we thought during the sixties and seventies. Therefore, the proliferation of lines of flight—suggested by Deleuze and Guattari as a means to emancipation—nowadays could lead us towards death. The task is to learn how to be and move in the world in an unexpected way and address a combination of multiple spatial-temporal scales and velocities to subvert and destabilize the hegemonic structures that subjugate humanity.

In "Deleuzian" terms, we have figured out how to proliferate black holes on white walls, and how to multiply white walls on black holes. We need to find the way to mobilize more lines of segmentations to organize ourselves, until we see the opportunity to penetrate the system from the back doors through lines of flight. That is what I call *the strategy of troubled river* or resistance *in medias res*. That's why Deleuze and Guattari state that the transformation shouldn't be too violent a gesture,

> since destroying the strata without prudence will drag us into a catastrophe. The worst thing then would not be to remain stratified—organized, signified, subject—but to precipitate the strata into a suicidal or insane collapse, which makes them fall on us, as a definite burden.[67]
> Only in this way, maintaining a meticulous relationship with the strata, is it possible to free the lines of flight, make the conjugated flows pass and flee ...[68]

In this context, Matéricos Periféricos' primary task in the context of design-build studios has been to help critical possibilities to germinate in order to break down little by little the continuity and wholeness of false hegemonic montages that prevent the development of a more just and equitable world. In this regard, we think that the sources of any possibility for novelty in the direction of creativity and emancipation from those false montages can be found only within the system's cracks, its fragments and remnants: the ruins, the trash, the buried bodies, and the stories of the losers and the oppressed. In this sense, design-build studios may be understood as the collective practices of decolonial design as they can help to locate, unearth, identify, and visualize those fragments and remnants, to discern ways to assemble them, to imagine alternative worlds from them, and, eventually, to coagulate them into artifacts. In this regard, our artifacts are community facilities co-constructed with the communities. They are conceived as orchestrations and the co-existence of emergent contents and expressions (matter-energies, forces, ideas, velocities, information, and variables of all kinds) that flow and are intercepted by our bodies that arrange and coagulate them into contingent and unstable multiplicities while performing in situ and in vivo actions.

Our design-build studios usually perform the co-construction of artifacts in order to underpin local institutions in their community activities, challenging state agency, returning public lands to the community, and activating small cooperatives and companies. They are community facilities, such as communal dining rooms, chapels, community centers, and sports infrastructure. They are also instruments for contributing to building community, supporting popular organization, and participating in activities that support collective self-awareness and emancipation processes. Artifacts are a physical manifestation of our interaction with those processes, as well as the coexistences, negotiations, and distillations of all participants' ideas, needs, dreams, and abilities. They don't have absolute presence because they are both historical manifestations and expressions of possible futures.

The mestizo, unfinished, and complex aspect of the artifacts reflects the material translations of tangible and intangible phenomena, but also a body of procedures capable of generating a collective dialogic co-construction. It is as if the artifacts had catalyzed those processes and contingencies. That is, they are open to those possible futures and becomings. They appear disruptive, uncomfortable, undisciplined, with overwhelming proliferations and accumulations. They are made with the materials that are at hand: dust; metal; donated, recycled, or discarded bricks; or even broken parts of other artifacts. Their forms do not correspond to the parameters of the aesthetics of the finished, or the search for a totality. They do not need a single story, a big idea, or a rationality that links structure-space-exterior facade in a linear way. There is no pre-figuration in the process of materialization. There is not an a-priori definition of the shape. Rather, there is an in situ, in vivo dialogic method that allows the co-existence of the opposite and the diverse, giving rise to new possible collective worlds. A world where all worlds happen. That's why the co-constructed artifacts could be defined as assemblages in movement or transformation and whose configuration at any time is a result of following contingency (rather than function), variables, accidents, and negotiations. The artifacts are a process of infinite present in which the correlation of forces is manifested through the orchestration of dynamics, the management of contingency, the expression of the available, and the amplification of the collective. The value of the co-constructed artifacts resides in the process, not in the product.

Finally, our artifacts have the ability to mutate or be informed by other materials and ideas. They are always a little bit torn, unfinished, and open, so that they allow new processes of mediation among heterogeneous elements, as well as further interpretations, mutilations, additions, while still retaining a certain degree of identity and consistency. In addition, many of the artifacts continue growing in space and matter; others are sectioned or modified; many are destroyed, burned, or disassembled. Some of their parts are translated or transported to other places and transformed or assembled into other things. A few of them just break apart, are taken over by nature, decompose, or become new raw materials. They also reverberate beyond their immediate physical environment. Some artifacts provoke additional infrastructural improvements in the neighborhood. Their physical presence forces public interventions or new and otherwise unimagined community works. After they are coagulated, the artifacts show behaviors that could be assimilated to an inner agency or vitality. In most cases, these artifacts function as a starting point for subsequent further processes of social and material change in the territory without the direct intervention of human beings. That is to say, they have their own agency.

1. bell hooks, "Theory as Liberatory Practice," *Yale JL & Feminism* 4 (1991).
2. See Matéricos Periféricos work at www.matéricosweb.com.
3. bell hooks, "Theory as Liberatory Practice," 1.
4. My translation from Paulo Freire, *Pedagogía de la indignación: cartas pedagógicas en un mundo revuelto* (Buenos Aires, Argentina: Siglo Veintiuno editores, 2012), 47.
5. David Harvey, *The 'New' Imperialism: Accumulation by Dispossession* (Oxford: Oxford University Press, 2003).
6. Cecilia L. Chu and Romola Sanyal, "Spectacular cities of our time," *Geoforum* 65 (2015), 399-402.
7. Julio Cortázar and Juan Fresán, *Casa tomada* (Buenos Aires: Ediciones Minotauro, 1969).
8. Julio Cortázar, *From the Observatory*, trans. Anne McLean (New York: Archipelago Books, 2011), 19-20.
9. Manuel DeLanda, *A Thousand Years of Nonlinear History*, eds. Jonathan Crary, Stanford Kwinter, and Bruce Mau (New York: Swerve Editions, 2000).
10. Gilles Deleuze and Félix Guattari, *A Thousand Plateaus: Capitalism and Schizophrenia*, trans. Brian Massumi (London: Continuum, 1998).
11. My translation from Ernesto Cardenal, *Los ovnis de oro: Poemas indios* (México: Siglo XXI, 1998), 48.
12. Cecilia L. Chu and Romola Sanyal, "Spectacular cities of our time."
13. Richard Falk, "Resisting 'Globalization-from-Above' Through 'Globalization-from-Below,'" in *Globalization and the Politics of Resistance, International Political Economy Series*, ed. Barry K. Gills (London: Palgrave Macmillan, 2000).
14. Manfred Max-Neef, "U.S. Is Becoming an 'Underdeveloping Nation,'" filmed in September 2010, https://www.youtube.com/watch?v=hjcbBnM2OUo.
15. Seo Bongman, "Borrowing Money: Aid, debt and dependence," in *A World of Difference: Encountering and Contesting Development*, eds. Eric Sheppard et al. (New York: Guilford Press, 2009), 559-93.
16. Faranak Miraftab, "Insurgent Practices and Decolonization of Future(s)" in *The Routledge Handbook of Planning Theory*, eds. Michael Gunder, Ali Madanipour, and Vanessa Watson (London: Routledge, 2017), 276-88.
17. My translation from Saúl Yurkiévich, *La movediza modernidad* (Madrid: Santillana, 1996), 336. In this excerpt he refers to Ernesto Cardenal's work.
18. Michael W. Jennings, Brigid Deherty, and Thomas Y. Levin, eds., *Walter Benjamin: The Work of Art in the Age of its Technological Reproducibility and Other Writings on Media*, trans. Edmund Jephcott, Rodney Livingstone, Howard Eiland, and others (Cambridge: Belknap Press of Harvard University Press, 2008), 25.
19. Jennings, Deherty, and Levin, *Walter Benjamin*, 25.

20. Theodor W. Adorno, *Teoría estética*, trad. Jorge Navarro Pérez (Madrid: Ediciones Akal, 2004).
21. Jennings, Deherty and Levin, *Walter Benjamin*, 24.
22. Ibid., 39.
23. Deleuze and Guattari, *A Thousand Plateaus*.
24. In that schizophrenic people do not separate their bodies from the world, and escape from a simplistic, triangular, Freudian interpretation of relationships child-mother-father, as well as from the mechanism of containing desire. For Deleuze and Guattari, we are all machines of desire.
25. In *Mille Plateaux* (the original French book) Deleuze and Guattari talk about *agencement* as the agencies, connections, and relations between components rather than as the specific way the components are physically assembled. It is from this agencement that strata, assemblages, or bodies without organs can emerge.
26. Manuel DeLanda, *New Philosophy of Society: Assemblage Theory and Social Complexity* (New York: Bloomsbury, 2019), 19. Also his lecture "A Comparison of Deleuze's Assemblage Theory and the New Materialist Approach" at Assemblage Thinking Symposium 2017, University of the Aegean, Dept. of Geography (GR) recorded and available at https://www.youtube.com/watch?v=VzJqOX4ASA8.
27. My translation from Godofredo Iommi M., *Carta del errante* (Valparaíso: Escuela de Arquitectura UCV, 1976), 9.
28. Jennings, Deherty, and Levin, *Walter Benjamin*, 30.
29. Cecilia Boal, professor and theater director who was Augusto Boal's partner for forty years says that the original title of the book Augusto Boal wrote was "Politic Poetics." Listen to her lecture at the Cycle "Critical 13/13. Critical theory texts. 13 seminars at Columbia." http://blogs.law.columbia.edu/critique1313/4-13/.
30. Augusto Boal, *Teatro del oprimido* (Mexico: Talleres Gráficos Continental, 1989).
31. My translation from Boal, *Teatro del oprimido*, 12.
32. B. H. Friedman, ed., *Give My Regards to Eighth Street: Collected Writings of Morton Feldman* (Cambridge: Exact Change, 2000), 87.
33. Lucretius, *On the Nature of the Universe*, trans. Roland Latham (Melbourne, London, Baltimore: Penguin, 1951).
34. Lucretius, *Nature*, 28.
35. Jane Bennett, *Vibrant Matter: A Political Ecology of Things* (Durham: Duke University Press, 2010).
36. Bennett, *Vibrant Matter*, xviii.
37. Manuel DeLanda, *New Philosophy of Society*.
38. Deleuze and Guattari, *A Thousand Plateaus*.
39. Deleuze and Guattari state that the difference between assemblages, strata, and body without organs is determined by the intensity of two variables: terri-

torialization-deterritorialization, and coding-decoding. High intensities of territorialization and coding tend to conform strata, and low intensities, body without organs. In the middle, assemblages.
40. Bennett, *Vibrant Matter*, x.
41. Ibid., xi.
42. Ibid., 54.
43. Ibid., 18.
44. Franz Kafka, "The Cares of a Family Man," in *The Complete Stories*, trans. Willa and Edwin Muir (London: Allen Lane, 1983), 428.
45. Bruno Latour, *Reassembling the Social: An Introduction to Actor-Network-Theory* (New York: Oxford University Press, 2005).
46. Bennett, *Vibrant Matter*.
47. Ibid., xvi.
48. Ibid., 9.
49. That is, the power of the whole is greater than the sum of its parts.
50. Bennett, *Vibrant Matter*, 21.
51. Such as mobilizing technical and political teams during the blackout to solve the situation.
52. My translation from Philippe Descola, *Más allá de naturaleza y cultura*, trans. Horacio Pons (Buenos Aires-Madrid: Amorrortu editores, 2012), 32.
53. Tim Ingold, "The textility of making," *Cambridge Journal of Economics* 34 (2010), 91-102.
54. Tim Ingold, "Materials against materiality," *Archaeological Dialogues* 14 (1) (2007), 1-16.
55. Ibid.
56. Tim Ingold, "The textility of making," *Cambridge Journal of Economics* 34 (2010), 91-102.
57. Ibid., 91.
58. Tim Ingold, *Being Alive: Essays on Movement, Knowledge and Description* (New York: Routledge, 2011), 89-95.
59. Ibid., 93.
60. EMBT Miralles Tagliabue, *Obras y proyectos* (Milan: Skira Editore, 2002).
61. Henri Focillon, *The Life of Forms in Art* (New York: Wittenborn, Shultz, 1948).
62. Deleuze and Guattari, *A Thousand Plateaus*, 47-81.
63. Deleuze and Guattari, *A Thousand Plateaus*.
64. Ibid., 359-433.
65. Deleuze and Guattari, *A Thousand Plateaus*.
66. My translation from Antonio Berni, Fundación Malba. Museo de Arte Latinoamericano de Buenos Aires. https://www.malba.org.ar/evento/antonio-berni-juanito-y-ramona/.
67. Deleuze and Guattari, *A Thousand Plateaus*, 165.
68. Ibid., 166.

Learning from Latin America

JOSÉ LUIS URIBE

1

In 2010, the exhibition *Small Scale, Big Change: New Architectures of Social Engagement* presented eleven projects and buildings located on the five continents. The exhibit was curated by Andres Lepik and showcased architecture that promoted a new way of inhabiting the built environment in peripheral and marginalized communities. The design and construction processes on show were developed through collaborative work between the architects and the residents, who identify themselves as articulating a process of social, economic, and political transformation that begins with small-scale works. Part of the exhibition press release states:

In addition to new modes of participatory design, the projects on display incorporate pioneering site-specific ecological and socially sustainable practices, including the exploration of both new and traditional materials. Populations that have previously rarely enjoyed the attention of architects are engaged in designs incorporating innovation worthy of the broadest attention. The renewed commitment of these architects and many of their colleagues to socially responsible architecture is reminiscent of the ideals of twentieth-century masters, but these designers eschew their predecessors' utopian, wholesale blueprints for change imposed from above. *Small Scale, Big Change* presents radically pragmatic, "acupunctural" projects—limited interventions with wide-reaching effects.

Reviewing the selection of works reveals a group of architects with a shared focus on formulating an architecture based on locally developed techniques as an operating logic in a context characterized by vulnerability and shortage. They establish an image of the architect as someone who articulates social change by means of a collaborative process based on artisan construction techniques, promoting low-tech architecture that acknowledges traditional building practices as a technical reference point.

Four years later, a similar approach was taken in the exhibition *The Architect Is Present* at the Museo ICO, Madrid, curated by Luis Fernández-Galiano. This exhibit brought together five international studios whose works pursue the objective of meeting societal needs while making best possible use of available resources.[3] The interest of the exhibition was focused on the value of humble and noble materials such as clay, bamboo, timber, and ceramic, which form part of an architecture that promotes a future based on local construction techniques. In the curator's own words:

> This exhibition presents the work of five influential international studios that have made austerity their ethical and aesthetic reference point. Covering the five continents, these young architects work in marginalized settings and demonstrate that limited resources can serve as a stimulus for technical invention and community participation, and the foundation of a responsible architecture where the vocation of service does not exclude beauty and emotion.[4]

Both exhibitions portray themes of shared interest among a specific group of contemporary architects, which opens up the discussion to the social purpose of architecture and the return of artisan values to construction taking place in marginalized contexts.

2

The above suggests that in the past twenty years, political circumstances and economic crises have oriented the contemporary architectural scene towards underserved contexts, promoting work that emerges in contexts of scarcity and is articulated by its abundant material resources. This condition has been examined in numerous publications, exhibitions, and conferences in the Global North that have focused on the Latin American condition of a post-crisis architecture. Reviews we could mention include: *AV Monografías* no. 138 (Latin America 2010-Spain 2009); *A+U* no. 532 (Latin America); *25 Projects* (Japan, 2015); and *Harvard Design Magazine* no. 34 (U.S., 2011).

To these may be added initiatives such as the versions of Freshlatino, Spain, 2009 and 2015, curated by Ariadna Cantis; the various versions of the Latin American Architecture Biennial (held in Spain); the symposium Latitudes, Architecture in the Americas (U.S.); and the Mies Crown Hall Americas Prize (U.S.). Each of these formats for dissemination and reflection on Latin American architecture share a common element in the practice of studios and collectives that ten years ago were considered emerging, such as a77, Argentina; Plan:b Arquitectos, Colombia; Al Borde, Ecuador; Lab.Pro.Fab, Venezuela; Lukas Fúster, Paraguay; and others. In this regard, the cover of the magazine *C3* no. 295, South Korea, 2009, eloquently portrays the process of territorial change Latin America is undergoing, with an issue dedicated to Medellín and Talca. These contrasting contexts offer, on the one hand, an account of a generation of emerging Colombian architects and, on the other, the formulation of an innovative academic model based on practice. In both cases, we recognize the construction of a territory and a focus on the architectural project associated with the public sphere.

Latin America is progressively defining a new architectural narrative, one that is guided by the impact of craftsmanship as an active part of buildings that foster public habitats. An architecture on the margins has emerged, articulated through small initiatives led by various architecture laboratories that have worked with communities, adding to debate around Latin America's contribution to the contemporary condition of architecture.

3

During the eleventh Ibero-American Biennial of Architecture and Urbanism, I had the opportunity to interview eighteen architects, publishers, and critics involved in the contemporary Latin American architectural scene. In a hotel room in the historic downtown area of Asunción, Paraguay, each of them answered a single question: "What does Latin America bring to the contemporary condition of architecture?"[5]

Carlos Quintas, former editor of the magazine *Obradoiro*, quoted the late Paulo Mendes da Rocha's claim that Latin America held the possibility of inventing the world.

Taking this line as a framework of action, a number of architecture schools from across the continent have played a fundamental role in reformulating the architectural landscape from the perspective of small-scale buildings designed and built by students in collaboration with small communities, training new architects in search of opportunities for projects better adapted to scarce resources. The role of the architect in society has been rethought, and a number of academic practices have emerged on the continent over the last ten years, including: Matéricos Periféricos, Argentina, 2001; the Graduation Studio of the School of Architecture of the University of Talca, Chile, 2004; the Al Borde Studio at the Indo-American Technological University, Ecuador, 2016; the Activo Studio at the Monterrey Institute of Technology (Querétaro campus), Mexico, 2010; and the Nubes de Madera Studio at the Architecture Faculty of the Pontifical Bolivarian University, Colombia, 2013.

4

Meanwhile, most of the architects and architecture firms that emerged in Latin America in the middle of the last decade have found academia to be a space of refuge and exploration, in light of the post-economic-crisis reality. The architecture of public buildings and second homes has been set aside, making room for entities that permit experimentation in project design and construction to emerge in marginalized community contexts. This is the reason why many of the projects built by academic practices across the region are located in impoverished contexts, in the reality described so exquisitely by Glauber Rocha in his manifesto *Aesthetics of Hunger* (1965):

> From *Aruanda* to *Vidas Secas* [Barren Lives], Cinema Novo narrated, described, poetized, discoursed, analyzed, aroused the themes of hunger: characters eating the earth, characters eating roots, characters stealing for food, characters killing for food, characters running away in search of food, ugly characters, dirty, ravaged, inhabiting ugly houses, dark and dirty. Such was the gallery of famished people that identified Cinema Novo with a miserabilism condemned by the government, by a critique that serves antinationalist interests, by the producers and by the public ...[6]

These are contexts familiar to the students, whose knowledge of this reality helps them to develop an architecture of resistance, one that is low-cost and small-scale but large in its social impact. Therein lies its complexity.

5

Latin American students have the experience of living in the places where they design and build, something that grants them the authority to experiment. It is not about constructing solely for the fascination of building, but formulating projects that address different dimensions, such as technical exploration or vulnerable social contexts. These conditions enable us to define the future Latin American architect as a mediator between the inhabitant and their cultural context. An architect who participates as an intermediary and who seeks to be associated with all the phases of the project, from direct interaction with the resident to participation in the construction process, promoting a collective spirit around the construction phase. This attitude inherent in a cooperative architecture can be identified in a number of peripheral contexts in Latin America, where architecture schools have independently developed academic practices based on reciprocity.

Following this logic, it is worth noting that this collaborative process between students and community is shaped by the materials that characterize a specific setting, as each architectural object gathers its material from this context, without ornaments, in a rough and sincere manner, expressing the honesty of earth, brick, and wood. However, this construction logic does not abandon altogether the exploration of contemporary materials associated with the artificiality of industrial production. Exploring materials opens up new technological possibilities for architecture, but conditioned by the economy of resources available. Unable to opt for advanced technology, the cheapest human resource appears in the form of the skills embedded in the hands of students after their constant training, in collaboration with design, digital, and physical tools. Regarding the latter, Juhani Pallasmaa has written:

> The tool is an extension and specialization of the hand that alters the hand's natural powers and capacities. When an axe or a sheath knife is being used, the skilled user does not think of the hand and the tool as different and detached entities; the tool has grown to be a part of the hand, it has transformed into an entirely new species of organs, a tool-hand.[7]

It is important to mention that all the constructions produced by the practical studios in Latin America are first-time works, and it is notable how defects arising from the use of recycled or waste materials acquire value as forms of architectural expression. Dribbles of mortar or repair patches are features of a handmade architecture that bring roughness and vibration to the surfaces of walls, roof slabs, and floors. These expressions of the process bring value to the haptic dimension of exploring each of the works that belong to this architecture. The surfaces are exhibited with the sincerity of an architecture without a skin. This allows us to appreciate the architecture emerging from Latin American academic laboratories as primitive, bearing in mind the words of Adrian Forty, who sees the concept of primitive as not politically correct and pejorative.[8] These are works whose beauty is rooted in their primitive character, a beauty of denigration that belongs to an architecture of the margins, with limited budget and recycled materials, contributing local value to contemporary architecture. This is why I believe that these architectural practices embraced by academia, rather than forming an architectural "scene," are instead a kind of ideological front. A front that cultivates an architecture of resistance, one that seeks to prevail against the models established by globalization.

6

To return to that room in the hotel in Asunción, Paraguay, Carlos Pita said the following about Latin America:

> Here I found there was something to grasp on to. There was an emotion in the care for the material and even in the understanding of a certain presence of the objects, a certain monumentality. I once read an interview with Sam Peckinpah from when he was screening *The Wild Bunch* in 1969. A woman accuses him of being too violent and explicit, and the director responds "Lady, did you ever see anyone shot by a gun without bleeding?" I think that Latin American architecture is an architecture that bleeds. It is an architecture that confronts reality, and above all transforms reality. The contribution of Latin America to the contemporary condition of architecture is the fact of being able to produce an architecture that is deeply rooted in the local. In the face of globalization and marketing, I think that Latin American architecture has the capacity to make space for itself. It smells of the soil.[9]

Thinking about Pita's words, it is worth noting that the value of academic practices in Latin America is based on constructive experimentation, where students, together with the community, explore technical innovation using a process of trial and error. This process reveals the risks taken by these laboratories of architecture in which each of their working processes takes each construction system to the extreme with the aim of exploring the formal, structural, and constructive possibilities of one particular material, without repeating repertoires used in earlier works.

1. The studios participating in this exhibition were: Diébédo Francis Kéré, Burkina Faso; Elemental, Chile; Noero Wolff Architects, South Africa; Anna Heringer, Germany; Michael Maltzan Architecture, United States; Hashim Sarkis A.L.U.D., Lebanon; Rural Studio, United States; Urban Think Tank, Venezuela; Jorge Mario Jáuregui, Brazil; Frédéric Druot, Anne Lacaton, and Jean Philippe Vassal, France; Estudio Teddy Cruz, United States.
2. Andres Lepik and Barry Bergdoll, *Small Scale, Big Change: New Architectures of Social Engagement* (New York: Museum of Modern Art, 2010), 4.
3. The studios participating in this exhibition were Diébédo Francis Kéré, Burkina Faso; TYIN Tegnestue Architects, Norway; Anupama Kundoo, India; Solano Benítez, Paraguay; and Anna Heringer, Germany.
4. Luis Fernández-Galiano, *The Architect Is Present* (Madrid, Spain: Avisa / Museo ICO, 2014), 7.
5. These interviews form part of *Ugly, Dirty and Bad: Looking at Contemporary Latin American Architecture*, a critical essay in audiovisual format. The project explores the current state of architecture in the region through the accounts of leading architects who gathered in Asunción, Paraguay, for the eleventh Ibero-American Biennial of Architecture and Urbanism in October 2019. Conceptually, the audiovisual account takes a reductionist approach: a limited number of well-known architects gathered in one place. A hotel room as location. Each is free to respond at will to a single question. A wide-angle, fixed shot is used. The direct ancestor of this audiovisual exercise is Wim Wenders's *Room 666* (1982).
6. https://www.documenta14.de/en/south/891_the_aesthetics_of_hunger_and_the_aesthetics_of_dreaming.
7. Juhani Pallasmaa, *The Thinking Hand* (Chichester: Wiley, 2009), 47-48.
8. Adrian Forty, *Primitivo, La palabra y el concepto* (Santiago, Chile: Ediciones ARQ., 2018), 9.
9. Extract from a recorded and transcribed conversation between Carlos Pita and José Luis Uribe, in Asunción, Paraguay, on October 8, 2019.

The Path of Community Learning

GUSTAVO DIÉGUEZ

In recent years, architecture teaching in Latin America has seen a proliferation of academic initiatives aimed at constructing full-scale projects. In light of their results, some of which are compiled in this book, the first question that arises is why have such experiences not been more common in the past?

In all likelihood, the emphasis on the autonomy of the project fostered by the most influential architectural theories of the past half century had some impact on the way that many universities chose to distance themselves from the tactile, material dimension of architecture in their project learning processes. This may also be the reason why the diverse means of architectural representation in all their variety retain complete control over the project concept, ignoring the opportunity to gain access to a more multidimensional experience, one that may even extend beyond the boundaries of the discipline. For this tradition of project-based teaching, the use of virtual tools and scale models suffices to meet its objectives.

What, then, is the potential of construction practices carried out in academic context, for learning architecture? If we focus on the structure of curricula, one argument in favor is the fact that real time materialization of design ideas proves to be an effective way of achieving the required verification of the academic learning that is scattered across the different course modules.

Criticism is often voiced in Latin American architecture schools regarding a dissociation between fields of architectural knowledge; technological content is separate from project design. The issue of the lack of integration among the different subject areas taught in the curriculum over the many years of an architecture degree is one that comes up time and again in evaluations of academic plans.

The close link between design and the experience of architectural construction enables the idea of the project to become an active part of the whole process. On this basis, students can understand the ideas of adaptation and resource optimization this task demands. The examples compiled in this anthology of case studies demonstrate from their multiple perspectives different specific ways of recognizing the built object as learning material.

In this context, this text should be understood as a cluster of ideas that emerged from the specific experiences gathered through this type of educational construction practice that we have been engaging in at a77 Studio.

On the path towards constructing the theory of a practice, the intention of this text is to highlight the nature of the opportunity that this pedagogical approach offers for architecture to play a mediating role in community learning about ways of inhabiting, making possible scenarios for reflection in order to find the greatest precision in each experience.

Carrying out site-specific interventions invites students and professors to observe their surroundings with care, and to understand the character of the resulting field of action. In this way, learning architecture emerges as an activity that reflects on shared ways of life. This pedagogical component gains greater relevance when we turn to look at situations of economic and social inequality. These experiences, which rely on collective learning, should address the delicate social responsibility that is inherent to them, and the political implications involved. As a result, new skills are required to carry out these processes, making it necessary to reformulate the notion of time implicit in the project, developing new networks and spheres of dialogue, building trust with communities, and producing new protocols that enhance added-value chains to the concept of collective construction.

The practice of technical skills, which is something expected by all architecture schools and assumed to be all that is necessary for the exercise of design, is rarely complemented by the practice of social skills, which treats design from another perspective: as a platform for production that establishes bonds among people.

By social skills we refer to the exploration at a technical level of formats for collaboration that are not limited to the standard idea of group work in university courses. Collective intelligence and collaborative attitudes are necessary tools for the construction of agreements and dynamics for liaising with the community that permit their real inclusion in the design and construction process. As a result, it is reasonable to suspend the idea that the design act is the fruit of an author-centered dynamic. This runs counter to a tradition that has consolidated the professional practice of architecture as a liberal activity whose meaning and the way of telling the story is determined by the author.

Those who find these experiences to be an opportunity for collective learning don't tend to establish closed procedures or fixed structures. These projects are rooted in specific local conditions that are not susceptible to systematization. Each social connection, each material expression, each fundraising effort demands its own most appropriate form in order to succeed.

The only sure factor that could encapsulate a methodological approach for such processes might be described as a tool: that of listening. Processes of conversation, listening, and interpreting operate here as a design strategy and as a mechanism for generating trust and attachment. The development of these projects requires an initial phase of public conversation and interviews, established as an exercise in approaching the issue and the problems to solve, as well as a way of understanding the future impact and the limitations.

The exercise in collective thinking we engage in consists of interpreting everything that we have heard during the conversations with the community, before developing a model that brings together the physical and infrastructural needs, the possibility of a phased construction, potential for future growth, flexibility and transformation of the spaces, and ideas about the maximum size of the planned work.

The purpose of involving community organization leaders and future managers and users of the spaces in the design and construction processes is to open up the discipline of architecture and foster a process of collective learning. In this way, we can boost trust and better target expectations. In this exercise of proximity to the community, communication normally acquires greater fluidity over the passage of the days. Listening ensures that the dynamic of mutual learning—through the exchange of experiences, the handling of tools and materials, and overcoming the inevitable challenges—enriches and forms an important part of the collaborative construction effort.

Building works that are imposed on a community tend to produce very little attachment, appropriation, and use for their intended purpose. This is frequently the case in public works built according to standard models and without communication with those who will occupy them. As a result, they end up prematurely deteriorated or abandoned. For this reason, it is important to schedule specific moments for sharing the work underway, where the community can offer criticisms, opinions, preferences, and where everything produced is then passed through a phase of integration of the ideas that have been highlighted, working with them in a collective exercise that synthesizes the program and allows progress to be made towards the definition of an architectural project.

Collective design-build studios enable students to enter into contact with construction materials and transform them in ways that test their design intentions. This moment is the result of a large number of preparations to ensure that each participant has a specific role to play, and establishes a considerable degree of responsibility and a sense of proximity to the work process and the results. The inclusion of members of the target community in construction processes extends this listening-based approach to all the project phases.

These academic experiences support the need to understand architecture as a logistical discipline, one based on management, movement of persons and materials, and the need to reach agreement. They also revive an ancestral component related to the collective act of construction as an event with an inspiring, almost mystical character, one that summons the strength of a social bond that is hard to obtain through other experiences.

What does it mean to make listening a central tool in the learning and practice of architecture? Developing the mediating capacity of architecture is only possible when we recognize its connections with other forms of knowledge and with the collective production of knowledge, without abandoning its place on the technical or formal plane. In this sense, listening is a political act because it entails putting into play a practice based on horizontal connections, the production of a dialogue that is transformed into a material object through the construction of a system of decisions. In the dissolution of authorship, the value of individuality does not disappear. To quote Jean-Luc Nancy:

> Community and communication are constitutive of individuality, rather than the reverse, and individuality is perhaps, in the final analysis, only a boundary of community. But community is no longer the essence of all individuals, an essence that is given prior to them. For community does not consist of anything other than the communication of separate "beings," which exist as such only through communication.[1]

The invitation to exercise architecture from a political perspective implies giving it a greater role in the development of management modalities and involving ourselves in the social dynamics of organizations and groups with an interest in improving their built environments. This brings into play the problematic characterization of political participation that Antonio Negri identifies in the context of the crisis of urban policies, and in the conceptual figures of the *urban laboratory* and the *political entrepreneur*.[2]

Through the replication of these types of studios and projects we hope that architecture may become a discipline for the people, mediating attachment and catalyzing community identity. Although in the history of Latin American cities there are examples that have achieved this, and that are included in this anthology, the great historical debt lies in the lack of popularity of this tool for social cohesion. Academic activity in deprived areas, through the construction of facilities and improvements to habitat, entails a new intellectual mold for the discipline and an aesthetic impact with a political dimension. It entails a high level of commitment to vulnerable communities in order not to disappoint expectations. It involves assimilating and understanding socio-environmental conditions.

> Neither sociological phenomenon nor ethnographic object: it is a vision from the crisis, an apprehension of the structures of normalized relations in the midst of perceptual collapse. ... It is a reversal of perspective: instead of deepening social analyses of the crisis, adopt the point of view of the crisis.[3]

The fundamental premise of all these ambitions lies in understanding architecture as a social good and a cultural product of the community that generates it. This criterion positions architecture as a discipline that, on the basis of its capacity and potential for the construction of identity, fosters the fulfilment of the human right to a decent habitat in the framework of meeting basic human needs.

1. Jean-Luc Nancy, "Infinite History" in *The Birth to Presence*, trans. Brian Holmes et al. (Stanford, CA: Stanford University Press, 1993), 154.
2. Antonio Negri, *De la fábrica a la metrópolis* (Buenos Aires: Editorial Cactus, 2020). "To positively address the problem of participation, perhaps it is necessary to take a step back. We need to reconsider a number of premises in our discourse. It is social cooperation that generates the conditions of production, the dynamics of appreciation, the material ties, and the interaction that coordinates and guides collective human action aimed at the production of goods and the reproduction of their conditions. It is on this basis that participation is determined."
3. Diego Sztulwark, *La ofensiva sensible: Neoliberalismo, populismo y el reverso de lo político* (Buenos Aires: Editorial Caja Negra, 2019).

Activo Studio (Monterrey)

Lab. Pro. Fab Studio (Caracas)

Nubes de Madera Studio (Medellín)

PEI Studio (Bogotá)

Atarraya Studio (Quito)   Al Borde Studio (Quito)

Four-teen Study Cases

E Studio (Asunción)

Travesías Studio (Valparaíso)   Matéricos Periféricos Studio (Rosario)   Intervención Comunitaria Studio (Santiago)

A77 Studio (Buenos Aires)   PAAF Studio (Buenos Aires)   Danza Studio (Montevideo)

Talca Graduation Studio (Talca)

FELIPE MESA
ANA VALDERRAMA
GUSTAVO DIÉGUEZ

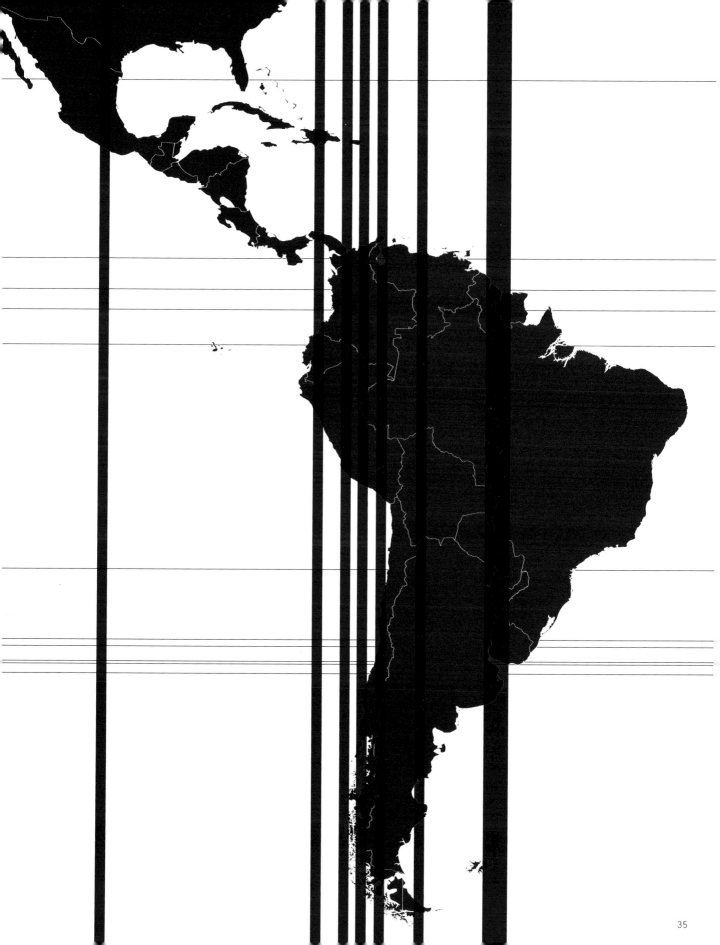

Travesías
Studio

Country:
Chile

University:
School of
Architecture
and Design at
the Pontifical
Catholic
University of
Valparaíso.

Professors:
Faculty and
assistants of
the School of
Architecture
and Design.

Duration:
1965/1984-2022

Studio timeline:
Forty-five
days in spring,
including the
calculation of
the journey,
the journey
preparations,
the journey, and
the construction
of the work.

Students:
Approximately
300 students
each year. The
school carries
out around nine
journeys per
year, organized
by the different
studios and with
around thirty
students taking
part in each
journey.

**Location of the
projects:**
South America,
from the Beagle
Channel to Easter
Island, the
Amazon, Ecuador,
the pampas, and
the jungle.

**Clients or
organizations:**
Municipalities,
communities,
schools,
universities.

**Donors and
financial support:**
Students,
faculty,
municipalities,
communities.

Publications:
School of
Architecture
and Design
e[ad]. Of note
are: *Amereida*
(Valparaíso:
Ediciones e[ad],
2011); *Amereida
Travesías
1984-1988*
(Valparaíso:
Ediciones e[ad],
1991); Alberto
Cruz, *El acto
arquitectónico*
(Valparaíso:
Ediciones
Universitarias
de Valparaíso,
2010).

The "Crossing the American Continent" Studio (Travesías Studio) emerged as a series of reflections and interventions initiated in 1952, after the creation of the Institute of Architecture at the Pontifical Catholic University of Valparaíso by Alberto Cruz and a diverse group of artists and architects: Arturo Baeza, Jaime Bellalta, Fabio Cruz, Miguel Eyquem, Godofredo Iommi, Francisco Méndez, José Vial, and Claudio Girola. The first, mythical journey, undertaken in 1965, was intended to embody an epic poem about South America through ephemeral installations, declamations, and discussions with the local inhabitants. On that occasion, a group of architects, poets, and philosophers left Punta Arenas and reached Santa Cruz de la Sierra, the place where the axes of the Southern Cross meet. In 1967 they published the book *Amereida* to collect the experiences of that first journey. In 1984 the school introduced the Travesías Studio as part of its curriculum and, since then, the eighteen school studios travel once a year during the spring.

During these journeys, faculty and students interact with diverse communities, and put into play the relationships between architecture and poetic word in an exercise of *being here and now*. The projects begin with the opening of the site, led by a poet who indicates the direction of the work. Then they develop exercises to measure and feel the space with the body, and shape it through experience. They build interventions collectively and openly, allowing adjustments, modifications, and evolutions.

The journey has a triple objective: travel, build, and donate. The journey brings students closer to a reflection on the territory of South America, emphasizing all the tasks necessary to carry out the journey and the project: the trip itself, food, work, finances, health, well-being, and the poetic aspect. Faculty and students practice reading the territory through observation, involving drawing and annotation. They build small infrastructures connected to the place, which entail halting the journey. They understand these constructions as poetic acts of an ephemeral nature at the service of the communities, and as gentle marks and signs in the landscapes, which express the performative act of learning by doing.

Year:
2017

Location:
Gala and Gaviota
communities.
Municipality of
Puerto Cisnes,
Aysén, Chile.

Area:
Twenty-four
square meters.

Students:
Sixty students
from the EAD PUCV
– Travesías 2017.

Professors:
Iván Ivelic,
Professor in
charge; Antonia
Scarella,
Assistant
Professor;
Bruno Marambio,
Assistant
Professor;
Maximiliano
Trigos,
Assistant
Professor;
Mauricio
Puentes,
Assistant
Professor.
Journey
preparation
by Professors
Alfred Thiers and
Felipe Igualt.

TASK: Build three emergency shelters—at twenty-three meters above sea level—for use by communities in the event of natural disasters.

SITUATION: The Aysén region has a large number of geological faults with sporadic seismic activity, high tides, strong storms, and landslides. In April 2007, a 6.2 magnitude earthquake caused landslides in the canal zone of the Aysén region, causing the death of seven people and the destruction of dozens of houses in the surrounding areas.

PROJECT: Based on the initiative of the residents, who built an initial shelter in the town of Gala, the work team confirmed the need to build three additional shelters, one in Puerto Gaviota and two in Puerto Gala. This journey involved travel, project management, and the transport of materials to the construction site at a height of twenty-three meters above sea level, in the mountainous topography of the region. The professors and students, spending time with the community and in alliance with the municipality, defined the best construction sites that were safe, accessible, and offered good views over the surrounding landscape. They designed and built cozy wooden shelters in modular form and adapted to the irregular topography. With balconies, terraces, and platforms, they expanded the interior space and connected these cube-shaped buildings with the surroundings.

Community:
Residents of the
communities of
Gala and Gaviota.

Program:
Three emergency
shelters.

Materials:
Foundations,
structure, and
wooden floors.
Ceilings
and walls of
corrugated zinc
sheets.

Cost:
US$10,000

Financing:
Municipality of
Puerto Cisnes,
Aysén, Chile.

Photography:
Iván Ivelic.

PUERTO RAÚL MARÍN BALMACEDA JOURNEY

Location:
Around Puerto
Raúl Marín
Balmaceda,
Municipality of
Puerto Cisnes,
Aysén, Chile.

Area:
Ninety square
meters.

Students:
Fifty-seven
students from
the EAD PUCV -
Travesías 2018.

Professors:
Iván Ivelic,
Professor in
charge; Antonia
Scarella,
Assistant
Professor;
Bruno Marambio,
Assistant
Professor;
Maximiliano
Trigos,
Assistant
Professor;
Mauricio
Puentes,
Assistant
Professor.
Journey
preparation
by Professors
Alfred Thiers and
Felipe Igualt.

TASK: Build an intervention that enables new activities in the Pioneros de Palena Plaza, which was an underused park, mainly due to the constant rains.

SITUATION: This project is an extension of the intervention carried out in the municipality of Puerto Cisnes in 2017, a town affected by seismic movements and tsunamis. On this occasion, the community and the municipality requested that students build a project in the existing public space in order to improve a number of areas, enabling the community to gather and engage in new activities.

PROJECT: The work team planned, designed, and built a system of platforms, pergolas, and roofs, connected to the existing paths and infrastructure—play equipment, tourist information booth—in the square. They transported the materials to the area, spent time with the community, and built ten roofed modules of nine square meters using a modular structure of beams and columns in treated pine, as well as seventy linear meters of walkway that allow the local inhabitants to gather and relax.

Community:
Residents
of Puerto
Raúl Martín
Balmaceda.

Program:
Civic plaza
and pergola.

Materials:
Modular
construction
using 2" x
8" treated
softwood.

**Financial
support:**
Municipality of
Puerto Cisnes.

Cost:
US$16,000

Photography:
Iván Ivelic.

PRAIA DO AMOR JOURNEY

Year:
2018

Students:
Thirty-three students from the EAD PUCV Travesía 2018 and students from the Federal University of São Paulo and the Federal University of Paraíba.

Professors:
Andrés Garcés Alzamora, Bruno Marambio Márquez, Mónica Duarte Aprilanti, internship professor at UFSP.

TASK: Jointly build an infra-structure that helps to restore the sources of work of the local fishing community.

SITUATION: The project sought to respond to the environmental and socio-economic problems of a fishing community in an abandoned port facility in the town of Paraíba. In recent years, the site had experienced the exponential growth of bars and small

Community:
Fishing
community of
Paraíba.

Program:
Fish market.

Materials:
Recycled wood and
plastic sheets.

**Donors and
financial support:**
Prefecture of
Conde.

Cost:
US$12,500.
Accommodation
and materials
provided by the
Prefecture of
Conde.

Photography:
Andrés Garcés
Alzamora.

informal stores on the tourist beach. The community was at risk of being eradicated. From the outset of the project, the Planning Secretariat of the Municipality of Paraíba began a series of meetings with the community, authorities, and community organizations to provide new spaces for fishermen, in coordination with the adjacent ecological park.

PROJECT: The work team designed nine shelters located along the dividing line between the coast and the exist-ing estuary. The students built these new spaces with a simple structure of columns, beams, and permeable enclosures in sustainable wood. The main sloping joists protrude from the volumes to generate covered eaves and larger shaded areas. Inside, fishermen can store their belongings and products for later sale.

Nubes de Madera Studio

Country:
Colombia

University:
School of
Architecture
and Design,
Pontifical
Bolivarian
University,
Medellín.

Professors:
Miguel Mesa,
Felipe Mesa.

Duration:
2013-17

Studio timeline:
Planning,
one month;
Design,
one month;
Development,
one month;
Construction
one month.

Students:
300 students
over ten academic
semesters.

**Location of
the projects:**
Municipality
of San Vicente
Ferrer and
municipality
of Támesis,
Antioquia,
Colombia.

**Clients or
organizations:**
Municipality
of San Vicente
Ferrer,
municipality
of Támesis,
Antioquia—Gloria
Giraldo.

**Donors and
financial support:**
Students,
professors,
municipalities,
Inmunizadora
Serye.

Publications:
Felipe Mesa and
Miguel Mesa,
Nubes de Madera
(Medellín:
Mesaestándar,
2017).

Nubes de Madera (Clouds of Wood) was the name that a group of professors and students gave to the set of projects they carried out in the Design-Build Studio of the Pontifical Bolivarian University in Medellín, in the years 2013 through 2017. This vertical studio for third- and fourth-year students saw the construction of ten small-format buildings in rural areas of the department of Antioquia, one each semester. In association with the rural municipalities of San Vicente Ferrer and Támesis, and with technical support from the local treated-wood construction company Serye, the course built cultural and educational buildings for vulnerable communities.

Each semester, a team of thirty students led by two professors—Miguel Mesa and Felipe Mesa—raised financial resources through raffles and donations. They built relationships with municipal leaders by identifying the needs of rural communities. The students designed various architecture options and developed the most interesting ones collaboratively, assigning specific tasks. They prepared work budgets and constructed small wooden buildings with the support of engineers, builders, and social leaders. They delivered buildings to the communities, exchanging time and knowledge. They brought to life a series of lightweight, permeable, and bioclimatic buildings that are also durable, low-cost, and low-maintenance. Treated wood was the main construction material: plantation-sourced, certified, and sustainable patula pine wood. They explored a structural system of columns, beams, and diagonal braces, connected with galvanized steel bolts.

This course sought to understand the notion of complexity in architecture as the process necessary to construct a building collaboratively, with all the phases and actors involved. For the professors, the completed buildings have both possible and necessary forms, and are also an expression of the constraints involved. The course placed more emphasis on collaborative work among students than on individual work, and gave greater importance to construction than to representation through drawings and models. In the words of Miguel Mesa and Felipe Mesa: "If a medical student must learn to treat a patient in a hospital, then an architecture student must learn to design, build, and interact with communities and clients in specific sites." In their view, it is important that students find a balance between architectural representation, design, and construction over the course of their careers.

COVERED COURTYARD

Year:
2013

Location:
House of Culture,
municipality
of San Vicente
Ferrer,
Antioquia,
Colombia.

Area:
Seventy square
meters.

TASK: Improve the common spaces of the House of Culture and repair the roof.

SITUATION: The stepped courtyard of the House of Culture was abandoned, in poor condition, and was being used as a store. Even the side that looked over the landscape was closed. The use made of the courtyard was minimal due to the climate of the municipality, where there is frequent rain.

PROJECT: The team proposed transforming the courtyard into an auditorium, renovating the floor to create a stone platform and building a new wooden structure—columns, braces, beams—to support a translucent roof that would allow use during rainy hours. Direct access of light was controlled by means of a new deep and permeable ceiling. The team demolished a wall that prevented views over the surrounding landscape and installed a new metal fence recycled from another construction. Children and adolescents from the municipality now use this space for musical rehearsals, theater, cinema, and classes.

Community:
Children,
adolescents, and
residents of San
Vicente Ferrer.

Materials:
Treated patula
pine wood,
galvanized
steel screws
and bolts, Royal
Veta stone floor,
polycarbonate
tile roof,
reinforced
concrete
foundations.

Cost:
US$15,000

Photography:
Alejandro
Arango.

COVERED WALKWAY

Year:
2016

Location:
Támesis,
Antioquia,
Colombia.

Program:
Covered walkway
for circulation
and events:
recess, classes,
games, etc.

Area:
Seventy square
meters.

Students:
Astrid Agudelo,
Víctor Ayala,
Andrés
Bobadilla,
Arantxa Cardona,
Sebastián
Casadiego,
María Guadalupe
Chamie, Fanny
Alejandra
Cujar, María
Isabel García,
Daniela Giraldo,
Estefanía
González,
Marcelo
González, Laura
González, María
Camila Londoño,
Juan David
López, Iván
López, Mauricio
Martínez,
Jheraldyne
Monsalve,
Valentina
Montoya, Manuela
Montoya, Juan
Esteban Moreno,
Juan Pablo
Muñoz, Rossana
Lizeth Murillo,
César Ortega,
Alejandra
Osorio, Jhoan
Sebastián
Prieto, Mariana
Ríos, Daniel
Rojas, Juliana
Valentina
Valencia.

TASK: Cover the existing circulation route between two classroom buildings to expand its use during rainy hours and recess.

SITUATION: Although it is an agricultural college with about forty hectares of land in which a large proportion of the academic activities take place outside—crops, cattle, stables, pig farms, chickens, etc.—the institution lacked covered outdoor areas to support recreation and activities—circulation, eating, games, etc.

Community: Students and faculty of the Víctor Manuel Orozco Educational Institution.

Materials: Treated [illegible] pine wood, galvanized steel screws and bolts, thermoacoustic tile roof, reinforced concrete foundations.

Cost: US$15,000

Photography: Alejandro Arango.

PROJECT: The work team decided to connect two classroom buildings via a covered walkway. They located the new wooden structure along an existing stepped walkway, supporting the columns over the garden, freeing up interior space. The new modular intervention of beams, columns, and diagonal braces took advantage of the existing slope, enabling it to be used not only as a broad corridor, but also as a place to occupy for classes, recreation, meetings, and civic events. The walkway modulates the external light and generates an elongated, habitable space, by means of permeable cladding, while following the overall geometry of the structure.

COVERED THEATER

Year:
2017

Location:
Botanical Garden, municipality of Támesis, Antioquia, Colombia.

Area:
Eighty square meters.

Program:
Covered theater for cultural events: concerts, theater, puppets, classes, etc.

Students:
Kelly Tatiana Alzate, Juan Camilo Alzate, Emilio Arango, Manuela Bedoya, Clara Castrillón, Marilyn Cataño, Dayana del Carmen Cotes, Juan Esteban Cruz, María Paulina Cuca, Silvana Dangelo, Mateo Díaz, Andrés Felipe Duque, Kevin Darío Escobar, Juan Camilo Guzmán, María José Mejía, Sofía Patiño, Armando Prasca, Sara Rodríguez, Diego Salamanca, María Adelaida Sánchez, Daniel Sarmiento, Ana María Suárez, Juan Pablo Úsuga, Sergio Valencia, Julián Vargas, Mario Vélez, Jorge Vélez.

TASK: Roof over the stage and the stands of an open-air theater inside the Támesis municipal botanical garden, allowing new activities and cultural uses.

SITUATION: The open-air theater in the botanical garden was underutilized due to the rainy climate. This prevented cultural events being held to complement visits to the botanical collections.

PROJECT: The work team decided to build a new roof for the outdoor theater. The challenge was to cover as much area as possible with a limited budget, locating all the columns to the outside, avoiding obstacles, and adapting the new wooden construction to the circular geometry and existing level changes. To achieve this, the students designed a structure with an octagonal plan with a central patio, eight perimeter columns, and a lightweight, near-flat roof. In this way, the new construction provides shelter from the rain, generates shade, and enables new activities—classes, conferences, talks, etc.—while maintaining close proximity to the garden.

Community:
Visitors to the
Támesis Botanic
Garden and
students.

Materials:
Treated patula
pine wood,
galvanized
steel screws and
bolts, asphalt
roof, reinforced
concrete
foundations.

Al Borde Studio

Country:
Ecuador

University:
School of
Architecture,
Indo-American
Technological
University, UTI,
Ambato.

Professors:
David Barragán,
Pascual
Gangotena,
Marialuisa
Borja, Esteban
Benavides.

Duration:
2015-17

Studio timeline:
Research, four
weeks; Design,
four weeks;
Prototyping,
four weeks;
Design
adjustment for
construction,
two weeks;
Construction,
four weeks.

Students:
125 students
over five
academic
semesters.

**Location of the
projects:**
Ambato, Ecuador.

**Clients or
organizations:**
Rural and
suburban
communities
and families of
students.

**Donors and
financial support:**
Students,
communities,
private
companies.

Al Borde Studio is the name that the Ecuadorian architecture firm of the same name has given to its academic participation in a number of universities in Ecuador, Peru, and Chile, under various formats and modalities. During the years 2015, 2016, and 2017, this group led a design-build studio at the Indo-American Technological University, UTI, located in Ambato, two hours from Quito. This studio, for fourth-year students, built over two and a half years more than fifty buildings or small-format interventions in outlying areas of Ambato and nearby rural areas.

Each instance of the course received twenty-five students who worked individually or in small groups, posing architectural design problems relating to their daily lives. To respond to the selected theme, they managed economic and material resources, involved family members and acquaintances, chose sites and programs, built and used the new spaces, all in a record time of four and a half months. Each project involved the application of varying strategies, the use of heterogeneous materials—bamboo, wood, metal, concrete, bricks, glass, straw, etc.—local technologies, and the development of lightweight programs: viewpoints, rooms, meditation spaces, reading spaces, among others. In some cases, students continue to use these constructions today, a situation that provides them with firsthand experience of carrying out maintenance, alterations, or extensions.

In its design-build studios at UTI, Al Borde emphasized work outside the classroom, trying to erase the difference between academia and professional practice. It asked its students to move outside of their comfort zone, making the best of situations with significant limitations to bring new projects to life. It invited the participants to confront everyday reality, understanding the architectural project as a positive challenge. Finally, it acted as a facilitator between the students and the community, stimulating work with the local people and the extraction of knowledge from habitual practices.

SHELTER FOR WAITING: QUILICO'S NEST

Year:
2016

Location:
Pelileo,
Tungurahua,
Ecuador.

Area:
Fifteen square
meters.

Program:
Shelter for
waiting.

Students:
Darío Cárdenas,
Jonathan Proaño,
Daniel Sandoval.

TASK: Build a shelter for paragliders who have to wait for indeterminate periods of time before taking off.

SITUATION: Before they can fly, paragliders must wait for favorable weather conditions, enduring cold and wind. To avoid accidents, both the top of the mountain they take off from and the landing site must be clear.

PROJECT: This group of students obtained permission from the owner of the site and the municipality to build a buried shelter at ground level, to accommodate paragliders and tourists. In this cuboid space, built inside the mountain, ten people can sit while enjoying the views of the landscape. With the help of paragliders and friends, the students excavated and built a wooden deck that maintained the original profile of the mountain, including its plant layer. With the help of a carpenter, they built a door out of wood and glass so the refuge could be closed while still allowing views of the outside.

Community:
Paragliders and
visitors.

Materials:
Earth, wood,
glass.

Cost:
US$250

Photography:
JAG Studio, Darío
Cárdenas, and Al
Borde.

SHELTER FOR SINGING

Year:
2017

Location:
Ambato, Ecuador.

Area:
Fifteen square meters.

Program:
Shelter for singing.

Students:
Mauricio Acosta,
Dennis Guerrero,
Adrián Sandoval.

TASK: Build a shelter for singing.

SITUATION: To overcome the shyness of a member of the group in the face of his desire to sing, the group decided to build a space with good acoustic qualities and open to the urban landscape, on a site donated by a relative.

PROJECT: This group of students designed a shelter in the shape of an urban megaphone, with a hexagonal geometry and open to the landscape. They built this enclosed, individual room for singing using a structure made of wooden slats, reinforced concrete foundations, metal plates, and recycled galvanized sheets. Its geometry not only aims to amplify the sound and open it up to the surroundings, but also to generate an intimate and safe space.

Community:
Students.

Materials:
Wood, reinforced
concrete,
metal plates,
galvanized
sheeting.

Cost:
US$500

Photography:
Jose de la Torre.

Year:	Location:	Area:	Program:	Student:
2016	Sucre, Tungurahua, Ecuador.	Fifteen square meters.	Shelter for studying.	David Guambo.

TASK: Build an isolated shelter for studying during the day, and for practicing guitar and listening to music at night without disturbing the family.

SITUATION: The student's grandmother owned a rural plot for growing potatoes. The upper part of the lot was made available by this indigenous family to build a small construction using local materials.

PROJECT: Using local building materials and techniques—wooden beams, columns, and floor; bahareque (bamboo and earth) walls; and straw roof—the student built a thirty-square-meter shelter on stilts. On the lower level, in contact with the grass, he proposed a meeting place for his relatives and the local farmers, and on the upper level he proposed a secluded and silent space to study, practice guitar, and enjoy the rural landscape. With the help of his family, he built this rectangular building with sloping roofs, and resting lightly on the topography. *Kusy Kawsay* means *passionate life* in Quechua, the language of the Andean indigenous people.

Community:
Students,
family, rural
community of
Sucre, Ecuador.

Materials:
Wood, clay,
straw, glass.

Cost:
US$1,000

Photography:
JAG Studio,
David Guambo.

Activo
Studio

Country:
Mexico

University:
School of
Architecture,
Monterrey
Institute of
Technology and
Higher Studies,
Querétaro
Campus.

Professors:
Alfonso Garduño,
director 2010-
15; Carlos Gómez;
Diana García;
Edmund Palaces;
Janna Castro;
Estefanía
Biondi, adviser
on social
participation.

Duration:
2010-15 directed
by Alfonso
Garduño; 2016-22
directed by
Edmundo Palacios.

Studio timeline:
Research and
preparation,
one month;
Design,
one month;
Development,
one month;
Construction,
one month.

Students:
150 students
over ten academic
semesters.

**Location of the
projects:**
Urban outskirts
of Querétaro.

Client:
Communities of
Querétaro.

**Donors and
financial support:**
University,
students,
professors,
communities,
donations
from private
companies and
individuals.

**Awards and
honors:**
First Prize,
Obras Cemex 2014,
in the Collective
Space category.
Projects
presented at the
Venice Biennale
2016, as part
of the Mexican
pavilion.

Activo Studio is the name of the design-build studio of the School of Architecture of the Monterrey Institute of Technology and Higher Education, Querétaro campus, directed by Professor Alfonso Garduño between 2012 and 2015. This course initially received third-year students and later welcomed more experienced fifth-year students. During this period, the studio built more than ten small-format projects in association with a number of neighborhood communities on the urban outskirts of Querétaro. The name of the studio expresses its interest in participatory architecture, with concrete and positive impacts for students and communities.

Each academic semester, the course received between twelve and fifteen students who worked in teams of three or four. During the first month they carried out field research and, advised by Professor Estefanía Bondi, came into contact with community leaders. In addition, they raised economic and material resources through parties, raffles, private donations, and support from the university. In the second month, they designed and presented project options to the community and to a large jury, which selected the most suitable proposal. From that moment on, during the third month, students and faculty worked together to develop the chosen proposal. In the fourth month they built the project with the help of companies, qualified workers, and local labor.

This course focused on ensuring that participatory processes, which often remain mere good intentions, lead to the construction of concrete projects, in line with the available resources. The groups always sought to offer the communities something more than what they expected from the project, with open, flexible programs, spatial and tectonic qualities, and simple but robust materials that require little maintenance. As the course built small-format buildings in the same area of the urban periphery of Querétaro, the work team planned these interventions as a form of urban acupuncture, with a larger-scale impact on the social fabric and the potential to transform the territory.

PERGOLAS AND STANDS
IN MENCHACA

Location:
Rio Moctezuma,
Santiago de
Querétaro,
Mexico.

Area:
120 square
meters.

Program:
Pergolas and
stands for the
soccer field.

Students:
Hans Duer, María
José Robles,
Alberto Meouchi +
Students Activo
Studio 2012.

Community:
Residents of
Menchaca 2.

Materials:
Metal structure,
reinforced
concrete
foundations,
wooden
platforms,
rocks.

Cost:
US$3,000

Advisers:
Gerardo Berumen,
Arturo Rios,
Guillermo
Lizardi.

Photography:
Yoshihiro
Koitani.

TASK: Build a shaded space to sit and watch sporting events on the existing soccer field.

SITUATION: The urban area of Menchaca 2, established more than twenty years ago as an irregular settlement, now has public services, but is also known for its high crime rates. The community requested the construction of pergolas and spaces to sit around the soccer field that functions as a public space for gatherings and sporting events.

PROJECT: The work team designed and built five rectangular, lightweight pergolas on one of the long sides of the soccer field. These metal structures, built with financial resources from the university, have reinforced concrete foundations and support wooden pallets donated by a private company. The Activo Studio initially built benches using bags filled with earth, but the climate soon destroyed them. For this reason, they moved large rocks from nearby to use as an embankment under the new structures. The social tension between different groups in the community is evident in this new space that is used intensely and on a daily basis, not only to watch soccer matches, but also for gatherings and recreational activities.

SOMBRERETE PARK
COMMUNITY CENTER

Year:
2013

Location:
Calle 43
Sombrerete,
Santiago de
Querétaro,
Mexico.

Area:
Approximately
180 square
meters.

In partnership with:
Cambridge
University,
Department of
Architecture,
Dr. Felipe
Hernández.
Cities South of
Cancer.

Program:
Community
center.

Students:
Octavio
Herrejón, Arturo
Rodríguez,
Nahim Magos,
Jordi Oriol +
Students from
Activo Studio
2013 + Students
from Cambridge
University
Department of
Architecture Y1,
Y2, Y3.

Community:
Residents of La
Esperanza.

Materials:
Reinforced
concrete
structure,
metal trusses,
concrete blocks,
metal roof tiles,
and translucent
tiles.

Cost:
US$15,000

Advisers:
Gerardo Berumen,
Arturo Ríos.

Photography:
Yoshihiro
Koitani.

TASK: Build a community center on the south side of Sombrerete Park.

SITUATION: In the Altos de San Pablo area, the community was already using an existing construction that was in poor condition for cultural events, classes, and gatherings. The community requested to replace this existing structure with a new project to carry out similar activities.

PROJECT: The new intervention consisted of the construction of a covered space for a range of programs—classes, gatherings, cultural events, etc.—as well as two lateral volumes with productive programs including a community kitchen and a recycling center. These two rectangular volumes, built in prefabricated concrete blocks, support metal trusses and a roof with opaque and translucent tiles. The metal structure also supports textile sheets woven by the community that function as translucent, colorful ceilings. The floor surface was built using concrete cylinders of the type used for resistance tests of reinforced concrete structures, and local stones. This permeable space, which hosts a large number of neighborhood and community events, generates constant political interest and debate, due to its social significance in the area.

VISTAS DE SAN PABLO CHAPEL

Year:
2014

Location:
Calle Vista
Azul, Santiago
de Querétaro,
Mexico.

Area:
124 square
meters.

In partnership
with:
Cambridge
University
Department of
Architecture,
Dr. Felipe
Fernández,
Cities South of
Cancer.

Program:
Chapel

TASK: Build a chapel on land previously donated to the community.

SITUATION: The site for the construction of the chapel, which consisted of a flat piece of land with excellent views of the city, was originally a sloping piece of land, leveled out by means of a cut and fill operation carried out without the necessary technical conditions.

PROJECT: Given the restrictive ground conditions, the work team decided to design and build a very lightweight chapel in wood, supported on a floating foundation slab in reinforced concrete. As a result, six wooden porticoes support a roof that slopes to the west to slightly reduce insolation in the afternoon. The pulpit of the chapel is located on the north side, avoiding direct sun falling on users during religious ceremonies. This permeable space also functions throughout the week as a classroom, dance hall, and community gathering place.

Students:
Daniela Cruz,
María José Robles
+ Students from
Activo Studio
2013 + Students
from Cambridge
University,
Department of
Architecture Y1,
Y2, Y3.

Community:
Residents of
Vistas de San
Pablo.

Materials:
Floor and
foundation slab
in reinforced
concrete;
porticoes and
structure in
wood, metal
tiles.

Cost:
US$7,500

Advisers:
Arturo Ríos,
Iñaki
Barrigamentería.

Photography:
Yoshihiro
Koitani.

a77
Studio

Country:
Argentina

Universities:
Institute of
Architecture and
Urbanism, School
of Habitat and
Sustainability,
General San
Martín National
University. a77
Studio seminar,
School of
Architecture,
Design and
Urbanism,
University of
Buenos Aires.

Professors:
Gustavo Diéguez,
Lucas Gilardi.

Duration:
2011-22. Academic
program active
since 2019.

Studio timeline:
Planning, between
three and six
months; Design,
between one and
three months;
Development,
between one and
three months;
Construction,
one month with
subsequent
completion
of work and
monitoring of
future stages.

Students:
Intensive
Studio modality,
approximately
twenty-five
students;
University
subject modality,
approximately
200 students per
year.

**Location of
the projects:**
Villa Hidalgo
and La Carcova.
Municipality
of General San
Martín, Province
of Buenos Aires.
Concordia, Entre
Ríos Province.

**Clients or
organizations:**
Social
organizations,
civil
associations,
foundations,
clubs, popular
libraries,
government
agencies and
institutions,
municipalities,
educational
institutions.

**Donors and
financial support:**
International
financing
agencies,
foundations,
companies,
university
support
programs.

**Awards
and honors:**
Argentinian
Solidarity
Architecture
Award;
Professional
Council of
Architecture
and Urbanism
(CPAU); and
Central Society
of Architects
(SCA), Urban
Intervention
category.
Selected for
BIA-AR 2014.
Finalist XII
BIAU, Teaching
Programs
category.

a77 Studio is an architecture team led by Gustavo Diéguez and Lucas Gilardi that develops a range of modalities and formats for the production of group design-build studios, with the participation of students in the construction of community facilities. Initially, they had experience with self-managed projects outside of academia and through open calls for multidisciplinary student participation. Subsequently, they carried out projects commissioned by state bodies with public funds. Currently, they alternate between projects for civil organizations and projects that they lead as professors in the design-build studios of two public universities.

In all cases, a77 Studio emphasizes a fluid dialogue with the community through a number of social dynamics— listening exercises and formulation of agreements— that allow collective knowledge to be developed about what is to be built, putting forward programs, phases, and available techniques.

In the cases organized for the university courses, the students' proposals emerge from a continuous dialogue with social organizations, including public presentations to the community. Sometimes the work teams select a single design that they then develop constructively; on other occasions, they integrate the best design ideas, producing a final version.

The members of a77 ascribe great importance to designing a logistics in which all participants interweave their functions. In their collective construction studios, usually held during vacations, they favor the construction of prefabricated pieces, which they then assemble to reduce construction times. The workdays, both in the studio and on the site, allow students to learn manual skills, the use of tools, and the ingenuity necessary to systematize the construction and the tasks required.

NECOCHEA CLUB

Year:
2011

Location:
Villa Hidalgo neighborhood, municipality of General San Martín, Province of Buenos Aires, Argentina.

Area:
Eighty square meters.

Students:
Twenty-five architecture students selected from a public call for participation.

Community:
Children and adolescents with their parents and members of the board of directors of the Eugenio Necochea Social and Sports Club. A total of approximately 200 children make up the club's teams.

TASK: Build a community meeting place. Build a concrete surface for children's sports, a playground for training, and a bleacher.

SITUATION: This project was an initiative of the Ministry of Infrastructure of the Province of Buenos Aires to provide small public facilities to vulnerable neighborhoods through a collective construction with the participation of students. The Necochea Club was the social organization with the greatest need in an underserved neighborhood. Based on conversations with the neighborhood organizations, the need arose to support the club that only had an area of land assigned to it, but no infrastructure.

Program: Plaza, community meeting space, and soccer field. Children's playground and bleachers.

Materials: Eucalyptus poles, threaded rods and nuts, eucalyptus strips and boards, corrugated zinc sheets, concrete foundations.

Cost: US$10,000

Institutions: Eugenio Necochea Social and Sports Club, Ministry of Infrastructure of the Province of Buenos Aires, Sustainable Urban Environmental Management Program (PMUAS); United Nations Development Program (UNDP).

Photography: Daniel Infante Liranzo and a77 Studio.

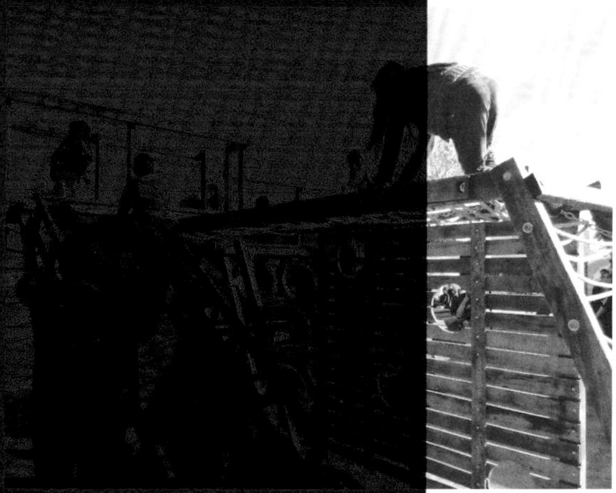

PROJECT: Initially, the work team defined the program with the club representatives, identifying as a priority the construction of a flexible space with a large roof to hold meetings and to offer food to children. They designed and built two modular and semi-hexagonal roofs, by means of parallel trusses and a system of eight double columns in eucalyptus wood, a material commonly used for installing telephone networks and cable television. They connected the structure with a system of threaded rods and fastening nuts that was easy to install and systematize. In this way, they simultaneously built the roof and the playing surface in ten days.
In a second phase, the work team designed a playground in collaboration with the children who attend the club. This project consisted of a wooden structure that functions as a bleacher, a climbing area, and a soccer training ground.

LA CARCOVA
EDUCATIONAL PARK

Duration:
Since 2019

Location:
La Carcova
neighborhood,
municipality
of General San
Martín, Province
of Buenos Aires,
Argentina.

Area:
200 square
meters.

Team of professors:
IA-UNSAM,
Argentina:
Claudio Ferrari,
Graciela
Runge, Roberto
Busnelli,
Gustavo Diéguez,
Lucas Gilardi.
a77 Studio
seminar (FADU-
UBA, Argentina):
Gustavo Diéguez,
Lucas Gilardi,
Florencia
Álvarez Pacheco,
Gastón Noriega,
María Rodrigues
Mori, Adriana
Guevara, Mario
Gagliano,
Gabriel
Monteleone.
Walter Gropius
seminar (FADU-
UBA/DAAD,
Argentina-
Germany): Markus
Vogl, Jens
Wolter, Juan
Pablo Negro. SuE
and IRGE seminars
(University
of Stuttgart,
Germany):
Markus Allmann,
Bettoma Klinge,
Sebastian
Wockenfuss,
Spela Setzen.
Matéricos
Periféricos-
Valderrama
Studio (FAPyD
and National
University
of Rosario,
Argentina), Ana
Valderrama.

Students:
Students of
the Design
Experimentation
Studio and the
Technological
Experimentation
Laboratory
(EHyS-IA-UNSAM);
a77 Studio
seminar (ADU-
UBA); Walter
Gropius seminar
(FADU-UBA-
DAAD); Matéricos
Periféricos-
Valderrama
Studio (FAPyD-
UNR); SuE and
IRGE seminars
(University
of Stuttgart,
Germany).

TASK: Build a community meeting space for the community of the La Carcova Educational Park.

SITUATION: The project for the La Carcova Educational Park arose from the development of a network of educational institutions interested in supporting vulnerable communities by holding collective construction workshops, in order to build small-format infrastructures. The La Carcova People's Library team was the dialogue partner in the territory for the development of the project.

Community:
La Carcova
People's Library
and residents of
the La Carcova
neighborhood.

Program:
Shade roof
and community
meeting place.

Institutions:
La Carcova
People's
Library,
German Academic
Exchange Service
(DAAD). STO
Foundation,
Aktion Palca
Foundation,
Municipality
of General San
Martín.

Photography:
a77 Studio.

PROJECT: The team of professors and students worked with the municipal policies for public space, defining a project to expand the library and a future strategy for the development of the existing educational park. It built consensus and trust with institutional actors and local people, and carried out the first intervention in the territory of La Carcova Park. The project consists of a large pergola that produces shade and defines a unique gathering place for the neighborhood community. This wooden structure was made up of eight columns, four parallel trusses, and three zigzagging roof strips, forming a flexible, permeable, and usable space. In the short term, and through new collaborative workshops, the interventions in the library and the park will continue, with the aim of building a children's center and a new sanctuary.

LUZ DEL IBIRÁ ENVIRONMENTAL EDUCATION CLASSROOM

Year:
2021

Location:
Concordia,
Province of Entre
Ríos, Argentina.

Area:
Sixty square
meters.

Students:
Thirty volunteer
students
selected from
a nationwide
call for
participants.

Community:
Students,
faculty, and
directors of the
Agroecological
Secondary School
and the Luz del
Ibirá Civil
Association.

TASK: Build an environmental education classroom in a natural environment linked to the Salto Grande Argentina – Uruguay binational dam.

SITUATION: This project, led by the Uruguayan organization Tagma, is part of a new network of sustainable classrooms in Latin America, built collaboratively following ecological principles—the generation of solar energy, water collection and treatment, the use of sustainable materials, etc. For the construction of the first environmental classroom in Argentina, Tagma initiated a participatory design process, involving a77 Studio and the ESFA Agroecological Secondary School community. Tagma understands the construction of this type of building as the best way to convey the premises of ecological activism.

PROJECT: The work team, working closely with the ESFA – Luz del Ibará community, proposed a rectangular building, located on the highest part of the land and oriented in a north–south direction for optimum bioclimatic functioning. On the first floor, they designed a flexible space to carry out educational activities relating to sustainability, while on the second floor they proposed a space for astronomical observation. Tagma and the community built mobile furniture to support these indoor activities. The new building has a semi-covered gallery to the east, a pergola to the west, space for a vegetable garden to the north, and bleachers to the south. These edges function as buffers against solar gain in the summer, favoring the growth of climbing plants that allow the sun to enter in winter. The work team used materials with sustainable qualities—plantation wood, airtight double-glazed windows, adobe walls, thermal panels—and water harvesting and solar power generation systems. The strategic location of this new construction allows it to function as an environmental classroom and as a public amenity.

Program:
Environmental education classroom for a secondary school specializing in agroecology.

Materials:
Structure of eucalyptus poles, prefabricated eucalyptus panels, eucalyptus floors and cladding, thermal sheet metal roofing panels, double-glazed windows, adobe wall, reinforced concrete foundations.

Cost:
US$15,000 + donations

Institutions:
Agroecological Secondary School (ESFA); Luz del Ibirá Civil Association; Tagma, Sustainable School Program.

Lab.Pro.Fab
Studio

Country:
Venezuela

Year:
2010

**Location of
the projects:**
Simon Bolivar
University
campus.

University:
School of
Architecture,
Simón Bolívar
University,
Caracas.

Professors:
Alejandro Haiek;
Carlos Ferré;
Sven Methling,
CearqUSB;
Henry Vicente,
Coordinator.

Studio timeline:
Preparation,
one month;
Design,
one month;
Prototyping,
one month;
Construction,
one month.

Students:
Twenty students
during one
academic
semester.

**Clients or
organizations:**
Communities
and students in
Caracas.

**Donors and
financial support:**
University,
students,
professors,
donations
from private
companies.

**Awards and
honors:**
Special Mention
VII Malaussena
Salon for
Architecture and
Urbanism, 2016.

Lab.Pro.Fab Studio is the name that Venezuelan architect and professor Alejandro Haiek gives to his design-build studios in various Latin American and international universities. Lab.Pro.Fab is also the name of his project laboratory, dedicated to the hybridization of traditional and new technologies, and to contemporary eco-social reflection. During 2010, Alejandro led a design-build studio at the Simón Bolívar University in Caracas. This course for third-year students focused on giving donated and unused materials a second life, building new spaces and prototypes that seek to enhance the well-being of the university community in the city of Caracas.

The studio received eighteen students who worked collaboratively for four months, studying the basic components of architecture: structure, floor, wall, and ceiling. The work team, advised by the university's construction shops, secured resources, evaluated construction techniques, and built modular components that it then assembled in a new space open to the academic community.

The Lab.Pro.Fab Studios emphasize the technical dimension and the artistic potential of architecture, fostering material experimentation and formal reflection in students, while also focusing on the social responsibility of the discipline. These courses are committed to immediate and quality architecture, introducing students to the emerging aesthetics of recycling, reuse, and hybridization.

SECOND LIFE PAVILION

Year:
2010

Location:
Campus of Simón Bolívar University, Caracas, Venezuela.

Program:
Outdoor classroom.

Students:
Alejandra Alonso, Amanda Álvarez, María Fernanda Arias, Mariandreina Baasch, Daniella Cavaliere, Claudio Cenedese, Cruz Criollo, Adriana Feuerberg, Mónica Fuentes, José Antonio García, Desiree Guédez, Alanna Kleiner, Rebeca Novoa, Michel Piñango, Hariadna Piñate, Denise Preschel, Gonzalo Romer, Irene Ruedas.

Community:
Community of students of the USB University.

TASK: Build an outdoor classroom on the university campus, using materials donated by private construction companies.

SITUATION: Various companies donated PVC pipes, metal profiles, plastic hoses, and cement. The university allowed the construction of the new pavilion in a forest close to the teaching areas.

PROJECT: The work team designed the various architectural elements using only the donated materials, which they transformed in the university construction shops. They built the floor using PVC cylinders that they filled with colored cement; they fabricated trusses with short tubes and metal joints; they erected permeable walls using plastic hoses; and they made the roof/pergola from PVC cylinders suspended from the structure. The combination of these irregular and colorful components gave rise to a transitory and welcoming space, open to the forest, and to the entire university community, for holding academic and festive events.

Area:
Thirty square
meters.

Materials:
Recycled pieces
of metal,
PVC, plastic,
concrete.

Cost:
US$1,000

Advisers:
Esteban
Tenreiro.

Photography:
Emanuel Cardoso.

PEI
Studio

Country:
Colombia

Duration:
1996-2022

**Location of
the projects:**
Palomino,
Guajira,
Colombia.

University:
School of
Architecture
and Design,
Pontifical
Javeriana
University,
PUJ, Bogotá.

Professors:
Carlos Hernández
Correa,
Director.
PUJ School of
Architecture
and Design
Professors:
Antonio
Yemail Cortés,
Christiaan Job
Neiman, Santiago
Pradilla
Hossie, Daniel
Feldman. Guest
faculty: Zoohaus
Platform,
Juanito Jones,
Liz Villalba,
Zuloark
Collective,
Manuel Pascual,
Luis Galán, Juan
Chacón.

Studio timeline:
Research and
preparation,
one month;
Design,
one month;
Development,
one month;
Construction
one month.

Students:
Approximately
300 students over
five academic
semesters
between 2010 and
2012.

**Clients or
organizations:**
Communities in
the municipality
of Palomino.

**Donors and
financial support:**
University,
students,
professors,
communities,
private
companies.

**Awards and
honors:**
First Prize,
Ibero-American
Biennial of
Architecture
and Urbanism
for the project
Palomino,
Society under
Construction,
Cádiz, Spain,
2012.

Karl Brunner
Prize for Urban
and Landscape
Design, 23rd
Biennial of
Architecture
and Urbanism,
for the project
Palomino.

Society under
Construction,
Armenia,
Colombia, 2012.

International
special mention,
Social Habitat
and Development
Category,
Pan-American
Architecture
Biennial, Quito,
Ecuador, 2012.

The PEI Studio is the International Studies Program of the School of Architecture and Design of the Pontifical Javeriana University in Bogotá, directed by Professor Carlos Hernández. This course, founded in 1996, has an interdisciplinary vocation and operates on the basis of intensive design workshops, led by a group of permanent faculty and national and international visiting faculty, who change in line with the themes addressed. The PEI receives an average of eighty architecture and design students per semester, who work collaboratively on a range of topics, constantly exploring new territories in the fields of art, architecture, philosophy, new technologies, and ecology.

During the years 2010, 2011, and 2012, the PEI worked in partnership with communities in the municipality of Palomino, in the La Guajira department of Colombia. Through a series of academic courses, visits, and workshops, which involved the participation of the Spanish collectives Zuloark and Zoohaus, and the open research and design platform Inteligencias Colectivas, the International Studies Program proposed a master plan of action, and implemented it with architectural projects of diverse nature and scale.

Palomino, Society under Construction, is the name of this intervention, in which a group of professors, students, community leaders, and advisers organized, de-signed, and built a variety of projects with sustainable qualities, using low-cost local techniques and materials. Thanks to diverse sources of financial support—both institutional and from professors and students—the work team was able to travel more than six times, establish a site presence, and join the community for variable periods of time. This enabled the construction of a network of small-format community and private infrastructures, focused on hygiene, rainwater collection, food security, and cultural and leisure activities: a new house of culture, a sports hall, bleachers for the soccer field, street furniture, water wells, and dry toilets, among others.

The PEI Studio believes in an interdisciplinary, international, collaborative, and open education in architecture. Mixing third- and fourth-year students, it places greater emphasis on key contemporary issues—new digital media, and eco-social phenomena—than on curricular and traditional aspects of the field of architecture. Its intervention in Palomino proposes a participatory and long-term teaching model, which involved living, building, and coexisting with vulnerable communities in their territories.

Duration:
2010-12

Locations:
House of Culture,
House of Sports,
Chamaco House,
Calixto House,
Basilia House,
Juan House, Jorge
House, Palomino,
Guajira,
Colombia.

Area:
Between five
and ten square
meters each.

Program:
Dry toilets
with rainwater
harvesting
systems and
irrigation.

Students:
Group of PEI
students
2010-12.

TASK: Build a network of infrastructures to address health, hygiene, and food-safety issues.

SITUATION: Faced with the lack of piped water and due to problems with septic tanks in poor condition and food security, there was a clear need to build ecological dry toilets for some communal buildings—the new House of Culture and the new House of Sports—and for some families in the area.

PROJECT: The work team decided to build a network of public and private toilets for the benefit of the entire community of Palomino, exploring various development, use, and maintenance options over time. These buildings are not only efficient models of dry toilets, rainwater harvesting systems, or infrastructures providing irrigation for small vegetable gardens, but also subtle interventions, with alternative spaces such as stands, small libraries, decks, pergolas, and balconies. All were built using stilt structures in native wood, walls made from traditional natural- and plastic-fiber frames, metal tile roofs, and water collection and distribution systems made from PVC pipes and recycled plastic containers.

Community:
Residents
of Palomino.
Families
of Chamaco,
Calixto,
Basilia, Juan,
and Jorge.

Materials:
Native wood,
bamboo, cane,
plastic fibers,
PVC, plastic
containers.

Cost:
Approximately
US$200 each

Advisers:
Sirimapa Group,
Orfelina Quinto,
Basilia Pérez,
Wilson Rincones.

Photography:
Juan Chacón.

HOUSE OF SPORTS

Location:
House of Sports,
Palomino,
Guajira,
Colombia.

Area:
Twenty-five
square meters.

Program:
Roofed
recreation
center.

Students:
Group of PEI
students
2010-11.

Community:
Residents of
Palomino.

Materials:
Wood, bamboo,
palm leaf,
braided plastic
fibers, braided
cane.

Cost:
US$1,000

Advisers:
Sirimapa Group,
Orfelina Quinto,
Basilia Pérez,
Wilson Rincones.

Photography:
Juan Chacón.

TASK: The community needed an office for Civil Defense, a public organization that in Palomino works with children and young people.

SITUATION: The available site that belonged to the community was located by the main soccer field. The elongated shape of the site had open space for a small building between the store and the existing native trees.

PROJECT: The work team designed an elongated and completely reversible building, with two spaces of the same size, the first one permeable, for meetings and classes; and the second one closed, to store books and sports equipment. For the structure, they built columns, double beams, and struts using recycled bamboo. They built timber foundations, and raised the wooden floor fifteen centimeters off the ground to prevent damp. Involving local labor, they built a roof out of native palm leaves with a geometry of hyperbolic curves, and erected walls woven out of colorful plastic fibers and woven cane stems. After a year, the community modified the initial program of the building, making it the new Palomino sports hall. Later, the work team built the dry toilet for this sports venue to the rear of the site.

HOUSE OF
CULTURE

Duration:
2010-11

Location:
House of Culture,
Palomino,
Guajira,
Colombia.

Area:
140 square
metres.

Program:
Cultural
infrastructure
for dance,
music, classes,
meetings,
religious
events, etc.

Students:
Group of PEI
students
2010-11.

Community:
Residents of
Palomino.

Materials:
Native wood, palm
leaf, concrete,
metal profiles.

Cost:
US$5,000

Advisers:
Sirimapa Group,
Orfelina Quinto,
Basilia Pérez,
Wilson Rincones.

Photography:
Juan Chacón.

TASK: Build a flexible cultural amenity for dance, theater, singing, and artistic activities.

SITUATION: The Palomino dance group needed a place to rehearse and perform for the community. The community action board made available the site for the construction of the new amenity, which involved local knowledge and labor in wood, concrete, and palm-covered structures.

PROJECT: The work team designed an open-plan and flexible rectangular space, defined by a smooth, reinforced concrete floor. They built a native wood structure using six perimeter columns, tie beams, and large roof trusses. Continuing the exploration begun in the House of Sports, they proposed a roof made up of two large volumes, implementing non-traditional geometries while maintaining the appropriate slopes for the use of palm leaves. This space, from which the Sierra Nevada de Santa Marta can be seen, today hosts dance, musical, educational, and religious events. As was the case with the House of Sports, in a second phase, the work team designed and built a dry bathroom, complementing the site services.

Matéricos Periféricos Studio

Country:
Argentina

Duration:
2001–22

**Location of
the projects:**
Metropolitan
Area of Rosario.

University:
School of
Architecture,
Planning and
Design, National
University of
Rosario.

Professors:
Faculty and
associates of
the Matéricos
Periféricos
Studio,
Valderrama
and Barrale
Seminars.

Studio timeline:
Concentrated
modality,
two months a
year; Expanded
modality, one
day every fifteen
days throughout
the year.

Students:
Approximately
200 students
each year.

**Clients or
organizations:**
Social
organizations,
civil
associations,
communities,
municipalities,
educational
and religious
institutions,
neighborhoods,
people's
libraries.

**Donors and
financial support:**
National
University of
Rosario calls
for continuing
education,
volunteers, and
technological
outreach;
provincial
and national
government;
private
companies,
communities;
students and
faculty.

Publications:
Matéricos
Periféricos
magazine, issues
one to sixteen
/ website: www.
matericosweb.com;
Ana Valderrama,
et al., *Poéticas
Colectivas*
(Buenos Aires:
Bisman Ediciones,
2018).

**Awards and
honors:**
Special mention,
SCA UNE Prize for
Solidarity 2020.
Distinction,
Solidarity
Architecture
Argentina CPAU
and SCA 2010.
First Barberis
Prize at the
BIAAR 2018.
Distinctions,
BIAAR 2016
and 2014.
Nine Arquisur
Extensión Awards
between 2010 and
2019. Creation
Grant from the
National Arts
Fund 2018.

Selected to
represent
Argentina at
the Venice
International
Architecture
Biennale 2018.
Distinction from
the Chamber of
Deputies of the
Province of Santa
Fe 2017, and
from the Chamber
of Deputies
of Argentina
2016. Special
Mention and
Distinctions,
National Award
for Sustainable
Architecture
and Urban Design
FADEA-Saint
Gobain.

Matéricos Periféricos is a collective aimed at contributing to socio-spatial justice in Latin American cities. It is made up of forty professors from the Rosario School of Architecture, as well as graduates and students who annually volunteer in design-build studios. Since 1997, Matéricos Periféricos has positioned itself in the peripheries, studying their social and physical patterns through research projects that yield maps, diagrams, and speculations. In 2001, with the major crisis in Argentina, the group decided to move to direct actions in the territory with the joint construction of community facilities carried out through design-build studios. Since then, these studios have been part of the work plan for the Barrale and Valderrama vertical courses, and two optional courses. The studios are developed in two modalities: a concentrated, two-month studio, from October to December; and an expanded studio, consisting of workdays distributed throughout the year. Depending on each project, students participate in all or part of the co-construction process.

The works of Matéricos Periféricos have diverse objectives, including supporting local institutions in their community activities, challenging state agency, returning public lands to the community, producing marks in the landscapes, and activating small cooperatives. During the design-build studios, the participants—students, faculty, and the community—co-manage and co-produce community artifacts and facilities. These are conceived of as mechanisms capable of catalyzing and manifesting—in their production process, space, and form—peripheral processes, materials, craft traditions, and social dynamics. Over time, some of the artifacts have brought about additional infrastructural improvements: their physical presence has forced public interventions that would not otherwise have occurred.

WATER PLAZA

Duration:
2014-17

Location:
Bajada Colacho,
Pueblo Esther,
Province of Santa
Fe, Argentina.

Area:
900 square
meters.

TASK: Co-build with the community a public space to share water and exchange produce from the river and the land.

SITUATION: The project is located in the upper part of a twenty-meter-high ravine, surrounded by a settlement of forty fishing families who needed an open space to share cultural and social activities and a space to sell the fruits of the river and the land.

PROJECT: The design consists of a series of concrete beams that zigzag between the trees, guiding the water and visitors through the gloom of the undergrowth, until the river is finally revealed. The path frames the landscape and, at the same time, provides a place to gather in the shade. The water is guided by the rustic reinforced concrete beams whose plasticity and incomplete, irregular surface suggest that the plaza has been created, like fossils, by the action of nature.

Professors, assistants, collaborators:
Patricia Barbieri, Claudio Pereyra, Eduardo Sproviero, Joaquín Gómez Hernández, Berenice Polenta, Pedro Ferrazini, Renata Berta, César Sant´Ana, Julián Sileiko, Flavia Císera, María Emilia Ambroa, Juan Amaya, Mariana Flor, María José Manzi, Belén Bonicatto, Selene Rizutti, Aneley Mansilla, José Di Pompo, María José Davico, Augusto Pila, Camila Ibarra, Victoria Barrale, Mario Alcocer, Lucía Frachetti, Rosana Lezcano.

Students:
Project Analysis One and Two students, Valderrama Studio, years 2014-17.

Institutions:
Commune of Pueblo Esther, National University of Rosario.

Community:
Bajada Colacho neighborhood, Pueblo Esther.

Materials:
Reinforced concrete with formwork made from recycled pallets. Bricks, metal profiles, corrugated metal sheeting.

Cost:
US$5,000

Photography:
Matéricos Periféricos.

COPA DE LECHE IN INDUSTRIAL NEIGHBORHOOD

Year:
2014

Location:
Granadero Baigorria, Argentina.

Area:
Fifty square meters.

Program:
Multi-purpose space for eating, education, and recreation.

Coordinating faculty:
Ana Valderrama and María Cortopassi.

TASK: Co-build a small community space with the future users.

SITUATION: The Copa de Leche food program functioned precariously in the homes of the mothers of the neighborhood children. This group of mothers called on Matéricos Periféricos to design and build a new flexible space to provide schooling, recreation, and dining activities for 150 children from the Industrial neighborhood.

PROJECT: The work team built a rectangular building, set diagonally in the backyard of a house, leaving a small patio to the north with the kitchen and entrance routes to the south. The roof shape reflects the interior spatial configuration, consisting of a small space for children to sit near the window, and a space with a higher ceiling for community activities. This arrangement produced a roof height close to the existing buildings on the south side, and a greater height in relation to the dividing wall on the north side, thereby permitting many hours of sunlight to enter in winter. Currently, following the formalization of the space, the state funds this food program.

Community:
Industrial
neighborhood.

Materials:
Structure in two-
by-six-inch pine
beams, membrane
in OSB panel,
polycarbonate,
and corrugated
metal sheeting.
Floor structure
in two-by-four-
inch C-profiles.
Reinforced
concrete
foundations.

Cost:
US$4,700

Photography:
Matéricos
Periféricos.

ITATI COMMUNITY SPACE

Duration:
2014-18

Location:
Villa Gobernador Gálvez, Province of Santa Fe, Argentina

Area:
Thirty square meters.

Program:
Flexible community space.

Coordinating faculty:
Marcelo Barrale, Rolando Supersaxco.

TASK: Co-build a small community space with the future users.

SITUATION: The new community space is located in a territory near the Paraná River, bordering the southern edge of a meat processing plant. It is a neighborhood with very dynamic processes of informal occupation and a high level of socio-environmental conflict. The project arose at the request of the nuns of the Santísimo del Rosario College.

PROJECT: The work team built a rectangular space, located on a diagonal to the site boundaries, in order to free up a pedestrian walkway leading to the inner neighborhood. The students designed tilting windows and wooden sunshades that encourage north–south cross ventilation, incorporating translucent sheets, arranged in respect of the views. They built a stepped concrete floor and aligned the roof with the natural slope of the land, responding to the configuration of the interior: a space available for meetings, classes, and artistic events.

**Professors,
assistants,
collaborators:**
Jorge Lattanzi,
Javier Elías,
Nicolás Cardone,
Carolina
Cardozo, Diego
Corghi, Pedro
Ferrazini,
Vanesa
Heisterborg,
Valeria Ríos,
Daniela
Sguazzini,
Santiago Marino,
Guillermo
Alfaro, Julián
Barrale, Aldana
Berardo, Evelyn
Patch, Franco
Capotosti.

Students:
Architectural
Project One
students,
Barrale Studio,
years 2014-18.

Cost:
US$4,000

Photography:
Matéricos
Periféricos.

TALCA
Graduation
Studio

Country:
Chile

University:
School of Architecture of the University of Talca.

Professors:
Eduardo Aguirre, Gregorio Brugnoli, Glenn Deulofeu, Kenneth Gleiser, Víctor Letelier, Andrés Maragaño, Juan Román, Susana Sepúlveda, José Luis Uribe, Germán Valenzuela, Blanca Zúñiga.

Duration:
Active since 2004

Studio timeline:
Definition of the site and research topic, two months; Definition of the general idea and the project, two months; Preparation of construction details, two months; Construction, two months.

Students:
The works are individual and around thirty are completed each year.

Location of the projects:
Central Valley of Chile.

Clients or organizations:
Social organizations, civil associations, communities, municipalities, public institutions.

Donors and financial support:
Companies, communities, municipalities, institutions, public grants.

Main publications:
José Luis Uribe Ortiz, ed., *Talca, cuestión de educación* (Mexico D.F: Arquine S.A. de C.V., 2013). Jose Luis Uribe Ortiz, ed., *Against the Tide: Chilean Pavilion at the 15th International Architecture Exhibition of the Venice Biennale* (Germany: Hatje Cantz, 2016).

Juan Román, ed., *Revistas Talca Nos. 1 to 5* (Chile: Editorial Universidad de Talca). Blanca Zúñiga Alegría, *Espacio público rural* (Chile: Editorial Sa. Cabana, 2021). Germán Valenzuela, ed., *Talca inédito* (Chile: Editorial Pequeño Dios, 2013).

Awards and honors:
Young Talent Architecture Award, Mies van der Rohe Foundation, Spain 2020. Global Award for Sustainable Architecture 2015, Cité de l'Architecture et du Patrimoine, France, 2015. Archiprix International, Hunter Douglas Awards, The Netherlands, 2017. Archiprix International, Hunter Douglas Awards, The Netherlands, 2012.

The School of Architecture of the University of Talca was founded in 1998 when the Council of Rectors approved the academic project prepared by the architect Juan Román. In 2001, the academic curriculum was defined, which to date continues to be organized into two semesters per year. The school's curriculum is based on three pillars: looking at the Central Valley of Chile as a territory for reflection and action; focusing on material culture; and *learning by doing* through design-build studios. Four types of consecutive and cumulative studios are held: first, the Materials Studio for first-year students, focused on an exercise with a cube of material; second, the Bodies Studio, also for the first year, deals with recognizing oneself in space and configuring the dynamics of movement; third, the August Studio or Work Studio, which sees students participate in building small-format projects in the Central Valley of Chile; and finally, the Graduation Studio, carried out by final-year students who must bring together the components of research, management, project, construction, and dissemination of the work.

In 2004, the first Graduation Studio was completed, as the most significant manifestation of the school's production and the graduate profile. The degree culminates with the project and the construction of an *in situ* work. The Graduation Studio is individual and requires students to define the prior conditions, get involved with the communities, build a network of relationships that allows them to mobilize energies so that the work happens, while managing and executing the material, financial, and construction possibilities of the work. The studio lasts eight months and begins in March with the definition of the site, the problem, or the research topic. In May and June, students develop the overall idea and the project. In July and August, they prepare the construction details and present the project to an evaluation group to request the "construction pass." Over the following two months they complete the construction of the work. Since the implementation of this program, the school has built more than 700 projects across Chile's Central Valley, which have served to strengthen community ties in the region.

DESCENT AMONG THE ROCKS

Year:
2017

Location:
Los Acantilados sector, Caleta de Pellines, Maule Region, Chile.

Area:
Eighteen square meters.

Program:
Descent Among the Rocks.

Student:
Angélica Méndez Poblete.

TASK: Provide access to the shore to collect seaweed.

SITUATION: The work is located on the steep, rocky descent to the shore in an area where coastal communities subsist by harvesting the products of the Pacific Ocean. The local population gather seaweed, and needed a better means of descending and ascending each day to facilitate access to the sea.

PROJECT: The student designed a route among the rocks, allowing descent and ascent without interrupting the landscape qualities of the area. The work consists of a very lightweight staircase built with two elements: a steel handrail that seeks the most favorable route between the rocks, and a series of strategically located oak wood steps.

Adviser:
José Luis Uribe.

Community:
Seaweed
gatherers
in Caleta de
Pellines.

Materials:
Steel, oak wood.

Cost:
US$150

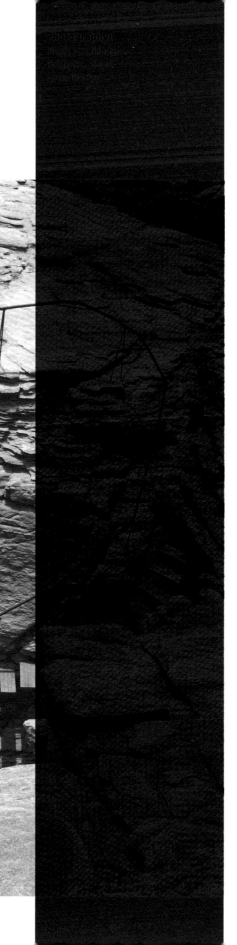

BLEACHER PLAZA

Year:
2019

Location:
Los Gomeros,
Pelarco, Maule
region, Chile.

Area:
100 square
meters.

Program:
Bleachers.

Student:
Sebastián
Quezada.

TASK: Build a gathering space and bleachers for the soccer field of the Los Gomeros Sports Club.

SITUATION: The work is located on the perimeter of a soccer field where there was already a pile of tires, some of them half buried and used as seats to watch the game.

PROJECT: The student took two pre-existing facts about the site as a basis for the project: the disused tires and the earth. He proposed the construction of an *animal made of tires* as a playful object to evoke the memory of childhood. He built the bleachers in the shape of a pyramid made up of a series of stacked and staggered tires that function as benches. In this way, he revitalized and encouraged the integration of the community in a previously underutilized space that was periodically flooded.

Adviser:
Glenn Deulofeu.

Community:
Los Gomeros
sports club.

Materials:
Tires, earth.

Cost:
US$120

Photography:
Miguel Salinas.

Year:
2018

Location:
Los Álamos, Maule
region, Chile.

Area:
Fifty-two square
meters.

Program:
Gazebo.

Student:
Enrique Moreira.

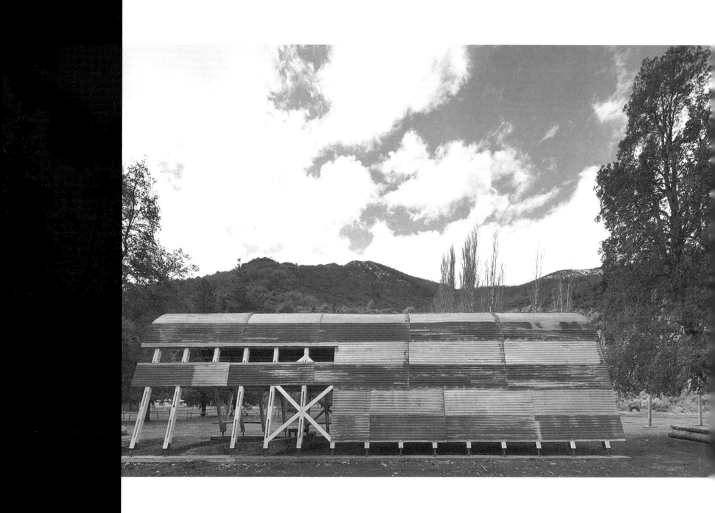

Adviser:
Andrés Maragaño.

Community:
Residents of Los Álamos.

Materials:
Reinforced concrete foundations, timber structure and metal ribs, recycled zinc sheets.

Cost:
US$750

Photography:
Federico Cairoli.

TASK: Build a meeting space based on a typological reformulation of the local shed design.

SITUATION: The project takes as its initial reference the vernacular architectures of the area, characterized by its serial structure, and establishes reciprocal relationships with the landscape by being built with local materials.

PROJECT: The student designed and built a shed with parabolic geometry, using parallel wooden "ribs," metal "nerves," and recycled zinc sheets. He placed this small building between two large trees, alongside the horse racing track used by the community, and built two parallel foundation beams and metal post bases to receive the structural ribs. On the open side towards the race track, he designed a V-shaped structure that enabled wooden benches to be installed for the community to enjoy the regular events.

PAAF
Studio

Country:
Argentina

Institution:
Higher School
of Architecture
and Design,
University of
Morón, UM-ESAD.

Current faculty:
Alejandro
Borrachia,
Dean; Alejandro
Albistur, Mabel
Modanesi,
Maximiliano
Larrañaga.

Former faculty:
Oscar Borrachia,
Jorge Barroso,
Carlos
Salaberry, Pablo
Itzcovich,
Gabriel Sottile,
Agustín Moscato,
Gastón Budin,
Vanesa Franco
Gómez.

Duration:
Active since 2016

Studio timeline:
Research and
project,
four months;
Planning,
two months;
Development,
one month;
Construction,
one month.

Students:
Between seventy
and eighty
students each
year.

**Location of the
projects:**
Mainly in the
Province of
Buenos Aires.

**Clients or
organizations:**
Government
institutions,
social
organizations,
communities.

**Donors and
financial support:**
Private
companies,
institutions,
chambers of
industry,
students.

Publications:
Vera Simona Bader
and Andres Lepik,
eds., *Experience
in Action!
DesignBuild in
Architecture*
(Munich: Detail,
2020).

**Awards and
honors:**
The Shelter
for Students
project in Jujuy
was included in
the exhibition
catalog
*Horizontal
Vertigo*, Venice
Architecture
Biennale 2018.
The PAAF Program
was declared
of interest by
the Chamber of
Deputies of
the Argentine
Nation.
Buenos Aires
Architecture
Biennial Prize
for new Academic
Practices. First
Prize Domus Lab
in the Research
category.
Recognition,
Fourth Edition
of the National
Award for
Sustainable
Architecture and
Urban Design,
organized
by FADEA and
Saint Gobain.
First prize for
solidarity by
an educational
institution,
awarded by the
Central Society
of Architects
of Buenos Aires
and FADEA.
Award at the
International
Architecture
Biennial of
Argentina
2018, Academic
Practices in
the category
technology,
crafts, and
industry.

The Federal Academic Support Program (PAAF) is incorporated into the architecture degree of the University of Morón as part of the Integrated Final Project, in which students manage, design, and build projects for specific recipients. This program is a university outreach policy that supports the construction of small-format community infrastructures for vulnerable communities. Initially, the students made contact with the communities, identified needs, and proposed the projects to be built. Later, working more systematically, the university made agreements with civil organizations to define projects with greater stability and impact. For example, an agreement with the municipality of Tigre, in the north of the Province of Buenos Aires, allowed 100 students to develop various projects in an underserved neighborhood. In that case, they built nine houses and a plant nursery, and developed improvements to the public space.

Currently, four professors lead the course, which emphasizes the following topics: management, technology, structure, design, works supervision, urban planning, and landscaping. In general, the interventions are small in scale, but in some cases they comprise strategies for a larger area. The program raises financial resources through architecture congresses and conferences, and secures donations of materials from private companies and municipalities. In many cases, the institutions served provide labor, and the students provide economic resources that they would otherwise invest in conventional design courses. The PAAF Studio supports the autonomy of its students and encourages them to respond to their curricular and social concerns through their built projects. It emphasizes a community-oriented and sustainable architecture.

STUDENT RESIDENCE IN JUJUY

Location:
San Miguel de
los Colorados,
Province
of Jujuy,
Argentina.

Area:
Forty square
meters.

Program:
Student
residence.

Students:
José Miguel
Lagues
Caballero,
Florencia
Tomalino, Marcia
Velázquez,
Cristian
Álvarez, Leandro
Pinheiro,
Leandro Iannaci,
Verónica
Brautigam, Lucas
Guerra.

Adviser:
Alejandro
Borrachia.

Community:
Residents and
students in San
Miguel de los
Colorados.

Materials:
Adobe, sand,
stone, cane.

Cost:
US$2,500

Photography:
Work team.

TASK: Build a housing module for young people who live far from the educational centers they attend.

SITUATION: San Miguel de los Colorados has two schools: Primary School No. 350 Malón de la Paz, with about thirty students; and 500 meters away, Secondary School No. 51, which has just over forty students. Many of these students live in remote places and walk up to five hours to attend class.

PROJECT: The work team, in association with municipal delegates, undertook the construction of a student residence using stone foundations and adobe bricks manufactured by the community. Taking advantage of local labor and technology, they proposed a building comprising two domes, with great structural stability and bioclimatic qualities. They located the dormitory in the dome with the largest diameter, and the social area in the smallest and highest. They designed circular skylights, allowing natural lighting of the spaces, and rendered and painted the exterior of the building in red, accentuating its function as a landmark.

MH3
LIBRARY

Year:
2017

Location:
Urban Nature
Reserve,
Sector 5B,
municipality of
Morón, Province
of Buenos Aires,
Argentina.

Area:
thirty five
square meters.

Program:
Public library
and lookout.

Students:
Ailin Casabene,
Natalia
Pieraccini,
Germán Rodríguez
Steinberg.

TASK: Build a public library in a nature reserve.

SITUATION: The municipality of Morón and the Higher School of Architecture and Design, University of Morón signed an agreement to permanently install a public library in the Urban Nature Reserve.

PROJECT: The work team proposed a modular building that is flexible and available for various uses and locations, which in this case was adapted to function as a library. Inside the first floor, they designed perimeter shelves to store books and a flexible space for reading and resting. On the second level, they created a semi-open terrace to observe the nature reserve. The participants constructed the building using prefabricated frames and wooden sheets donated by private companies, using a modular system that made the best use of secondhand materials. The students finished the building using a vinyl tarpaulin that delicately covers the terrace.

Community:
Residents of the municipality of Morón and visitors to the nature reserve.

Materials:
Structure of columns and beams in Paraná pine wood, galvanized steel pile foundations, metal anchors, tarpaulin upper lining, interior linings and furnishings in phenolic plywood and pine wood slats.

Cost:
US$2,500

Advisers:
PFI Seminar.

Photography:
Work team.

PLANT NURSERY AND DINING ROOM

Year:
2018

Location:
Tigre, Province
of Buenos Aires,
Argentina.

Area:
Sixty square
meters.

TASK: Construct a small building for plant cultivation and community gatherings.

SITUATION: The traditional culture of self-production of food in the Tigre community has been gradually disappearing. The project aims to reincentivize this practice.

PROJECT: The participants proposed the construction of a modular building with a hybrid program, which simultaneously allows for the cultivation of plants on the second level and for the community to meet around an open dining room on the first level. In order to build on an island, they designed a wholly prefabricated building, transporting all the sections on a boat. They built a mixed structure of wooden columns and metal beams, and to guarantee cross ventilation and the entry of natural light to the crops, they enclosed the building with openable wood and polycarbonate panels. Additionally, they integrated the building into its context with an elevated platform to avoid future flooding problems.

Community:
Families
of resident
islanders in
Tigre.

Materials:
Pine wood
structure,
panels and
mezzanines,
phenolic
plywood, wooden
floors and decks,
metal beams
and anchors,
metal stairs
and railings,
alveolar
polycarbonate
sheets,
reinforced
concrete
foundations.

Cost:
US$2,500

Advisers:
PFI Seminar.

Photography:
Work team.

Intervención Comunitaria Studio

Country:
Chile

University:
School of
Architecture,
University of
the Americas,
Santiago de
Chile.

Professors:
Juan Pablo
Corvalán,
Professor
and Dean of
the School of
Architecture;
Leandro
Cappetto,
professor;
Julio Suárez,
director.

Duration:
Active since 2016

Studio timeline:
Joint analysis,
one semester;
Joint design,
one semester;
Joint
implementation,
one semester.

Students:
Twelve students
each year.

**Location of
the projects:**
Santiago de
Chile, Villa
Músicos del
Mundo.

**Clients or
organizations:**
Communities of
Villa Músicos
del Mundo and San
Joaquín.

**Donors and
financial support:**
University,
students,
professors,
communities,
donations
from private
companies.

Publications:
Fernando Portal,
ed. *Academia
como práctica*
(Santiago de
Chile: Ediciones
Academia
Espacial, 2020).

The Community Intervention Studio is a degree course of the School of Architecture of the University of the Americas in Santiago de Chile, part of a multidisciplinary program of community interventions developed by the university. In this modality, the course works with city neighborhoods to propose interventions connected to the needs of their inhabitants. To achieve this, a small group of students—between ten and twelve participants—works collaboratively and individually for a year and a half with faculty, advisers from other schools, and neighborhood organizations. In 2021 and 2022, a group of six students worked in Villa Músicos del Mundo, and proposed an Architecture Festival in the neighborhood as a closing event, with six small-format architectural interventions, mixing playful activities, urban art, and celebratory performances. This latest version of the Graduation Studio, which the professors named *Fantasies in Uncertainty*, was developed over three academic semesters. In the first, the students prepared a group analysis and jointly developed the intervention with the community, obtained economic support, and narrowed down the programs; in the second, they designed their projects in the neighborhood individually, while continuing their dialogue with the community; and in the third, they jointly implemented or built the new spaces. The university supported these interventions with economic resources—up to one-third of the total value of each project—and the students raised funds through raffles and donations.

This studio, which is still in operation today, understands academia as a critical spatial practice, and the built project as a mediating instrument between the pedagogical processes and the socio-environmental phenomena of Santiago's neighborhoods. It treats architectural design as a multidisciplinary and collaborative process, aimed at the construction of common goods. It encourages social programs that go beyond the immediate needs of the communities, inviting reflection and the unexpected.

THE DYNAMIC HOUSE

Duration:
2021-22

Location:
Plaza Chile/
Debussy, Villa
Músicos del
Mundo, Santiago
de Chile.

Area:
Thirty square
meters.

Program:
Stage for plays,
puppets, cinema,
space for
classes, stall
for sales, among
other uses.

Student:
Rachel Molina.

TASK: Build a permanent and flexible space to support the public activities of the community in Plaza Debussy.

SITUATION: During the Covid-19 pandemic, the need for a flexible space to accommodate and stimulate leisure and recreational activities in the neighborhood was evident.

PROJECT: The work team decided to place the new intervention adjacent to one of the dividing walls of the existing houses, to maintain the traditional form and avoid occupying the open space of Plaza Debussy. The student designed this new playful infrastructure as an open stage available for various programs: puppet theater, open-air cinema, children's games, sales stand during the weekend fairs, and a place to rest. With a simple wooden structure—columns, beams, diagonal braces, wooden floor, and gable roof—the construction expands and welcomes the public life of the neighborhood. Its bright blue color functions as a festive signal in the public space.

Cost:
US$750

Adviser:
Luis Leiva,
Structures
Workshop.

Photography:
Sebastián
Mejías, Bárbara
San Martín, Juan
Pablo Corvalán.

BENEATH THE METROPOLIS

Duration:
2021-22

Location:
Metro Rodrigo de Araya, Vicuña Mackenna Avenue, Villa Músicos del Mundo. Santiago de Chile.

Area:
Fifteen square meters.

Program:
Metropolitan spatial manifestation, habitable space beneath the Santiago elevated metro.

Student:
José Acuña.

TASK: Identify an abandoned space where an architectural operation can be deployed that links the neighborhood with the large metropolitan infrastructures around it.

SITUATION: The abandoned and neglected space under the elevated metro has the potential to become a provisional urban stage, open to the community as an architectural performance, intensifying the perception of and questioning the problems of daily life in the neighborhood.

PROJECT: The work team designed the intervention beneath the reinforced concrete structure of the elevated metro in Santiago, opposite a bus stop. In this way, the project, made up of a wooden bridge running parallel to the elevated viaduct and two translucent curtains hanging from the elongated structure, acts as an urban stage to be viewed and occupied. The bridge, which enables passage over some existing concrete barriers, occupies the place, makes it visible, and invites the community to inhabit it. The long curtains intensify the sense of a passage, giving shape to the stage. The red color of the wood and the curtains, and its contrast with the gray of the urban landscape, mark out the underutilized space and draw attention to the place in a festive way.

Community:
Residents of
Villa Músicos
del Mundo.

Materials:
Red textile,
rope, red
painted wood.

Photography:
Sebastián
Mejías, Bárbara
San Martín, Juan
Pablo Corvalán.

PRODUCTION TO THE LIMIT

Duration:	Location:	Area:	Program:	Student:
2021-22	Franz Schubert and Gluck streets, Villa Músicos del Mundo, Santiago de Chile.	Thirty square meters.	Stage for an urban play.	Katherine Roa.

TASK: Build a mobile stage for the presentation of urban plays in the neighborhood.

SITUATION: The Covid-19 pandemic revealed the need for festive, artistic, and collaborative events in the Los Músicos neighborhood.

PROJECT: The work team built a mobile stage for the performance of plays that involve the community as both spectators and actors. This lightweight, modular wooden construction can change places, occupying street corners, platforms, front gardens, and streets within the neighborhood's urban fabric. The structure has two hollow columns that support a raised platform and cantilevered trusses from which fabrics and objects can be hung, expanding the possibilities of the stage. The purple color of this permeable structure contrasts with the typical colors of the neighborhood, endowing it with uniqueness and a festive character.

Community:
Residents of
Villa Músicos del
Mundo.

Materials:
Purple painted
wood.

Cost:
US$740

Adviser:
Luis Leiva,
Structures
Workshop.

Danza
Studio

Country:
Uruguay

University:
School of
Architecture,
Design and
Urban Planning,
University of the
Republic, FADU–
UdelaR.

Professors:
Marcelo Danza,
professor;
Marcelo
Staricco,
coordinator.
Teaching
team: Lucía
Bogliaccini,
Germán Tórtora,
Marcos Guiponi,
Ximena Villemur,
Victoria Abreu,
Macarena Trías,
Patricia
Carriquiry,
Sebastián
Olivera.

Duration:
Active since 2011

Studio timeline:
Design,
management, and
development,
three months;
Construction,
one week.

Students:
Approximately
100 students for
each semester
course.

**Location of
the projects:**
Montevideo.

**Clients or
organizations:**
Municipality of
Montevideo.

**Donors and
financial support:**
The projects are
financed with
contributions
from the students
through the
sale of food and
beverages, their
own funds, and
donations.

Publications:
Revista Mapeo
"Especies de
Espacios"
(2016),
Montevideo,
Uruguay. Taller
Danza vol. 15
*Placer en la
Disciplina*
(2016),
Montevideo,
Uruguay. Taller
Danza.
Folders 3
"Reflexión en la
Acción" (2022),
Montevideo,
Uruguay. Comisión
Sectorial de
Investigación
Científica, CSIC,
Universidad de
la República
Vol. 03.

The Danza Studio is one of the nine seminars in architectural design at FADU–UdelaR, which offers courses in all years of the architecture degree. During the first year, this studio engages in experiences of collective construction. The exercises are, in general, interventions in the public space previously defined by the faculty in collaboration with municipal authorities. The interventions, carried out as a team by faculty and students, aim to intensify the use of underutilized public spaces through ephemeral works of architecture for periods of time ranging between one and three months. To fund the projects, the participants form a cooperative, each contributing the cost of what they would normally invest in a conventional design studio. In some cases they also receive donations and other contributions.

In each version of the course, the faculty distribute the work among five teams of approximately twenty students. Each group develops a number of projects over three weeks and selects the most interesting one. An external jury then chooses the project that will be built from among the proposals of each group. The chosen project becomes everybody's, and the teams are then organized into commissions by area of interest: prototypes, construction details, lighting, media, and logistics. After a month spent working on project development, the participants, led by the prototype team, build the project collaboratively in a week and inaugurate it together with the communities.

The professors of Danza Design-Build Studio place their focus on transitory and lightweight architectures that have the ability to trigger new uses and programs in the consolidated public space of the city, often disused or abandoned. They understand architecture as a public or collective event. Through modular and changing geometries, students propose interventions that energize the city and encourage the reappropriation of public spaces by citizens.

THE CLOUD

Year:
2015

Location:
Plaza Ex Terminal
Goes, Goes
neighborhood,
Montevideo,
Uruguay.

Area:
200 square
meters.

Students:
Introductory
course students
of the Danza
Studio.

Community:
Residents of
Montevideo.

TASK: Temporary intervention in the Plaza Ex Terminal Goes, triggering new public activities.

SITUATION: The public space around the Centro Cultural Goes had fallen into disuse and lacked good lighting at night. Existing industrial structures offered opportunities for an intervention to generate new activities in their shadow.

PROJECT: The work team collaboratively developed and built the ephemeral project *The Cloud*, which consisted of a volume hanging from the existing industrial structure, with a new lighting system. The participants prefabricated the new structure in the school's shop, building wire ribs stiffened with tubular aluminum rods that were then covered in plastic mesh, generating an irregular volume. Inside it, they designed a lighting system of T5 fluorescent tubes in series—connected to the public streetlight timer circuit—which functioned as an enormous lamp illuminating the public space at night. During the day, *The Cloud* went unnoticed, but after dark, its eighteen-meter-long volume, floating above the floor of the Plaza de la Terminal, encouraged community meetings, gatherings, and conversations. After two months, *The Cloud* was transferred to the Spanish Cultural Center in Montevideo, and became an itinerant project.

Program:
Ephemeral
installation in
public space.

Materials:
Aluminum tubes,
wire, PVC
fabric, green
fluorescent
paint.

Cost:
US$2,000 +
donations

Photography:
Marcos Guiponi.

Year:	Location:	Area:	Students:	Community:
2016	Plaza de la Diversidad Sexual, Montevideo, Uruguay.	350 square meters.	First-year students of the Danza Studio.	Residents of Montevideo.

TASK: Temporary intervention in the Plaza de la Diversidad Sexual in the old city of Montevideo, enabling new public activities.

SITUATION: The Plaza de la Diversidad Sexual was in disuse. The empty space and the hard floor surface offered opportunities for an intervention to occupy the area and generate new public activities.

PROJECT: The work team collaboratively developed and built the ephemeral project *Celeste*, which consisted of a set of lightweight modular structures to introduce shade, color, and lighting to the square, hosting new activities, walks, and routes. The participants prefabricated these modules with circular-section PVC pipes, providing stability and support with heavy concrete bases. The installation occupied the surface of the plaza through the repetition of a homogeneous material, alternating joints at ninety degrees, and strips of lighting to allow it to be used at night.

Program:
Ephemeral
installation in
public space.

Materials:
PVC tubes and
joints, lights,
concrete bases.

Cost:
US$2,000 +
donations

Photography:
Marcos Guiponi.

125

Location:
Plaza Zabala,
Montevideo,
Uruguay.

Area:
180 square
meters.

Students:
First-year
students of the
Danza Studio.

Community:
Residents of
Montevideo.

TASK: Temporary intervention in the Plaza Zabala in the historic center, triggering new public activities.

SITUATION: The crowded public space of Plaza Zabala suggested an intervention with new artificial lighting and a temporary roof to create a meeting place.

PROJECT: The work team developed, designed, and built an ephemeral pergola within the square. This new elongated and branching structure generated shade between the trees and artificial lighting at night, allowing greater use of public space. The participants manufactured the new structure using a braced system of Allround multidirectional scaffolding, clad in translucent white textile, and longitudinal lighting on the main beams. The forty-meter roof forked between the trees, accompanying the path of passersby and generating new spaces for citizens. The students inaugurated the new space together with the community and dismantled the project after a few months.

Program:
Ephemeral
installation in
public space.

Materials:
Tubular
scaffolding
structure,
translucent
plastic fabric.

Cost:
US$3,000 +
donations

Photography:
Marcos Guiponi.

E
Studio

Country:
Paraguay

University:
School of
Architecture,
Design and
Art, National
University of
Asunción.

Professors:
Lukas Fúster,
Sergio Ybarra,
Guido Enrique
Yambay.

Duration:
2018-20

Studio timeline:
Design and
development,
three months;
Construction:
three weeks.

Students:
Thirty students
for each semester
course.

**Location of
the projects:**
Asunción,
Paraguay.

**Donors and
financial support:**
The projects are
financed with
contributions
from the students
through the
sale of food
and beverages,
swaps, and
donations
of leftover
materials.

E Studio arose from the initiative of four professors—Juanchi Giangreco, Lucho Elgue, Javier Corvalán, and Solano Benítez—who were looking for alternative teaching methods. This vertical course was planned as a seminar lasting the entire degree course, emphasizing different aspects of the architectural project in each semester. During the years 2018, 2019, and 2020, with a group of thirty students in each course, professors Lukas Fúster, Sergio Ybarra, and Guido Yambay led the third semester of the seminar, focusing on the study of structures in architecture and their tectonic and formal qualities. Initially, they built large models in concrete, wood, and spaghetti that were subjected to load tests. Subsequently, they gathered funds and materials to construct small-format buildings for the benefit of the university community.

Each semester, the students worked in ten groups, securing resources, defining relevant programs, and de-signing projects with different materials and structural qualities. After evaluating various options, they chose the best proposal to develop collaboratively, dividing up the different functions: budgeting, purchases, details, construction, etc. The constructions were carried out intensely over a period of three weeks, and are a subtle balance between the abstraction required to understand the structural and constructive implications at stake, and the desire to connect the project with the university context of the campus and the city.

This course emphasized not only architectural design, but also the importance of understanding that projects have technical, sustainable, and management aspects. This meant that the contact with donors and users, and with construction tools and materials, was decisive in the academic process followed by students and teachers.

HAMMOCK

Donations
Annals de la 2018

Location:
National University of Asunción, Asunción, Paraguay.

Area:
Twenty square meters.

Professors:
Lúkas Fuster, Sergio Ybarra, Guido Martínez, Diego Soto, Viviana Pozzoli.

Students:
Santiago Alonso, Ámbar Arce, María Ayala, Araceli Bogado, Alina Cantero, Rodrigo Carrera, Paula Chamorro, Diego Díaz, Lissandre Dos Santos, Carlo Escobar, Vanina Estigarribia, Larissa Flores, Guadalupe Gaona, Fiorella Garay, Lourdes Gómez, Lara González, Belén González V., Catherine Granada, Fiorella Greco, Camila Ibarra, Trinidad Itza, Gabriela López, Sofía Omella, Gisella Portillo, Rocío Ramírez, Mikaela Ríos, Yessica Rodríguez, Edgar Rodríguez, José Trinidad.

Community:
Academic
community of
the university
campus.

Materials:
Recycled
pine planks,
metal joints,
nautical ropes,
reinforced
concrete
foundations.

Program:
Rest module
for students.

Cost:
US$400

Photography:
Federico
Cairoli.

TASK: Build a rest module for rural communities of horticulturists, putting it to the test in the context of the university campus.

SITUATION: Initially, the project was intended for a rural context, but during its development the decision was made to build it on a one-to-one scale for the student community on the university campus.

PROJECT: Participants conceived of this project as a meeting and rest space, inspired by the tensioned structural system of hammocks, their characteristic rocking, and minimal weight. Using wooden planks from donated shipping crates, they built a braced structure with four supports anchored to reinforced concrete foundations. Connecting the wooden trusses by means of metal plates, they generated the necessary rigidity to withstand the movement and tension of a network of polypropylene ropes that hang from the points of greatest stability. These meshes produce a sequence of spaces at different heights, casting shade on the ground surface where traditional plants can grow. The participants conceived this rest module as a replicable project in different areas of the campus and in rural areas near the city.

OBSERVATORY

Duration:
August–December
2018

Professors:
Lukas Fúster,
Sergio Ybarra,
Guido Martínez,
Viviana Pozzoli.

Community:
Academic
community of
the university
campus.

TASK: Build an observatory and rest area for students on an unused terrace of the university campus.

SITUATION: Initially, the project was conceived of as an astronomical observatory located in an isolated context. It was then developed as a new space for observation and relaxation on the university campus.

PROJECT: The work team located the project on a previously unused terrace, and built a staircase to permit new activities there.

The participants designed a permeable structure by reusing metal and galvanized-steel profiles to construct three inclined columns that support an external system of trusses with a square plan, and an internal system of trusses with an octagonal plan. The project takes the form of a twisted cube that is accessible to users and creates a polygonal window looking up at the sky and a focal area for observation.

Students:
Saida Aid,
María Gabriela
Arrom, Ronald
Ayala, Camila
Bogado, Ulises
Caballero,
Andrea Cabañas,
Fátima Cáceres,
Vanessa
Castillo,
Larissa Chávez,
Adrián De
León, Kathia
Fernández,
Néstor
Florenciano,
María Elsa
Gayoso, Dalma
González,
Alejandra
Hermosa, Minerva
Martínez,
Alejandra
Mereles, José
Miranda, Nadia
Moral, Camila
Morinigo, Alexa
Ocampo, Pía
Pappalardo,
Emilia Piris,
Damaris Racchi,
Martín Ramírez,
Marcos Ramos,
Lourdes Resquin,
Francisco Rodas,
Cielo Rodríguez,
Gabriel
Rubio, Desiree
Splinder,
Larissa Torres,
Esteban
Traverzzi,
Mauricio Vargas.

Program:
Astronomical
observatory and
pergola.

Materials:
Recycled
galvanized
profiles from
transmission
towers, leftover
light steel
profiles for dry
construction,
polyethylene
textile.

Cost:
US$700

Photography:
Federico
Cairoli.

AGUJERO DE VYSOKA

Duration:
March-July 2019

Location:
La Chacarita
neighborhood,
Asunción,
Paraguay.

Area:
250 square
meters.

TASK: Restore and intervene a formerly private construction to turn it into a cultural and community space.

SITUATION: The curators of the eleventh Ibero-American Architecture and Urbanism Biennial in Asunción decided to take advantage of the ephemeral event to develop a permanent cultural building for the city that would outlast the biennial.

PROJECT: The work team proposed restoring a dilapidated private house to use as an exhibition space during the architecture and urbanism biennial, and in exchange for the renovation, the owner agreed to allow the community use of the space for five years, for plays and cultural events. The participants worked on the design for four months and built for a month and a half in collaboration with La Escuela Taller of the municipality of Asunción, which is dedicated to teaching manual trades. They secured resources through swaps, donations, and the reuse of existing materials in the place. They reinforced the main walls with new mixed columns of wood and galvanized-iron profiles, and used the same materials for the construction of bridges that cross the rooms and connect the spaces. They held cultural events to raise funds for the installation of an air conditioning system that expanded the uses of the building.

Asunción
School Studio
professors:
María Emilia
González, Marcos
Zorrilla, Sergio
Cogliolo, Carlos
Gaona, Vicente
Cristaldo.

Community:
Residents of the
La Chacarita
neighborhood.

Headquarters of
the Paraguayan
Pavilion for
the eleventh
Ibero-American
Architecture
and Urbanism
Biennial based in
Asunción.

Materials:
Wooden columns
and galvanized
profiles from
transmission
towers, recycled
timber floors,
recycled ceramic
floor tiles,
steel deck slabs.

Cost:
US$6,500

Photography:
Federico
Cairoli.

Atarraya
Studio

Country:
Ecuador

Universities:
Munich University of Applied Sciences, MUAS; Portland State University, PSU; University of Tokyo, UT; University La Salle Oaxaca, ULSO.

Professors:
Lorena Burbano and Sebastián Oviedo in association with other faculty.

Operation:
2017-20

Studio timeline:
Research, fundraising, design, and work plan, three months; Construction, five weeks.

Students:
Forty students over four academic semesters.

Location of the projects:
Ecuador and Mexico.

Non-academic organizations:
Opción Más, Campo A.C., Municipality of Chamanga, communal, ejido, and municipal authorities of Santa Catarina Quiané.

Donors and financial support:
Students, communities, organizations, universities, municipalities.

Awards and honors:
Chamanga Cultural Center, Shortlist Fibra Award 2018/19. Stuttgarter Leichbaupreis 2018. Panamerican Biennial of Quito 2018. Selected, National Prize, Social Habitat and Development Category. SEED Award 2018, Winner, excellence in Public Interest Design; Deutsches Architecture Museum 2020. Quiané Center for Culture and Ecology, Panamerican Biennial of Quito 2020. Finalist, World Prize, Social Habitat and Development category. Special Mention, Fritz Höger Award 2020.

Atarraya Studio is the name of the action and research studio of Ecuadorian architects and Professors Lorena Burbano and Sebastián Oviedo. It is intended to collaborate with social organizations, public bodies, and educational institutions, and is aimed at fostering participatory processes of habitat production, together with communities, collectives, and movements across Latin America. Between 2017 and 2018, they worked with the Chamanga-based organization Opción Más, Portland State University, the University of Tokyo, and the Munich University of Applied Sciences to develop, design, and build a cultural center with students in the community of San José de Chamanga, a fishing village seriously affected by the earthquake that Ecuador suffered in 2016. During 2018 and 2019, they taught at the Munich University of Applied Sciences—under the direction of Professor Ursula Hartig—to manage, design, and build with students a center for culture and ecology in association with the community of Santa Catarina Quiané, in Oaxaca, Mexico.

Each of these projects received an average of twenty students who worked as a team with faculty, advisers, and community leaders to manage resources, design the cultural centers, and build them in two phases.

In the first year, American, Japanese, and German students traveled with professors to Ecuador, and in the second, German students and professors traveled to Mexico, where they joined local students. On both occasions they lived with the communities during the construction period, combining local techniques, available materials, and curricular knowledge. The new buildings have simple, welcoming, and permeable geometries and spatialities.

The name *atarraya* (meaning "cast net") refers to fishing culture, and is a metaphor for the fabric of relationships that constitutes social and spatial interventions. In its courses and projects, Atarraya Studio addresses all project activities including management, design, and construction. It works with organizations whose political approach is based on the contributions of different types of knowledge and actions, trying to demystify academic knowledge as the only truth.

CHAMANGA CULTURAL CENTER

Duration:
2017-18

Location:
San José de Chamanga, Muisne, Ecuador.

Area:
180 square meters.

Community:
Residents of San José de Chamanga.

Program:
Cultural center for dance, theater, music, training, classes, etc.

TASK: Manage, design, and build a cultural center for the local organization Opción Más.

SITUATION: Since 2009, the local organization Opción Más has led cultural programs for children and young people, focused on recovering and strengthening their Afro-Ecuadorian and Montubian (coastal farmer) heritage. After several years of activity, the house they used for their programs was destroyed by an earthquake in April 2016. In response, Opción Más and Atarraya, in association with other Chamanga-based actors, led a process of research, participation, and implementation for a new cultural center. It brought together Portland State University and the University of Tokyo to participate in the design and construction of the first phase, while the Munich University of Applied Sciences spearheaded the second phase.

PROJECT: Working on a lot between party walls measuring nine-by-fifteen meters, the team designed a project with two parallel bars, configuring a double-height central atrium, open to the community, and integrated into the public space. Using traditional materials and techniques, the team connected the building to its surrounding context. They built the ground floor in brick and reinforced concrete, generating protection against humidity, structural stability, and security. The second floor was built using lightweight structures in wood and bamboo, permeable enclosures in bamboo, and the roof from recycled polyaluminum sheets. This diverse group of people also built a rainwater collection and storage system, and dry composting toilets. Opción Más and other groups from Chamanga use the cultural center today for workshops on art, film, music, and ecology, and for neighborhood assemblies.

Materials:
First floor—
foundations,
floor, and
structure in
reinforced
concrete, brick
walls. Second
floor—structure
and walls
in wood and
bamboo. Recycled
polyaluminum
sheet roofs.

Cost:
US$33,000

Photography:
Santiago Oviedo.

QUIANÉ CENTER FOR CULTURE AND ECOLOGY

Duration:
2018-20

Location:
Santa Catarina Quiané, Oaxaca, Mexico.

Area:
Phase One, 200 square meters; Phase Two, 230 square meters; Total, 430 square meters.

Program:
Cultural and Ecology Center.

Community:
Residents of Santa Catarina Quiané.

TASK: Develop, design, and build a culture and ecology center on communally owned land.

SITUATION: Fighting to maintain communal ownership of their land, the Front for the Defense of the Land, together with the municipal, communal, and ejido authorities of Quiané, sought to build a new center for culture and ecology, in association with the organization Campo. The Munich University of Applied Sciences was invited to participate in the design and construction of this space through its design-build studio. The project consolidated community initiatives, strengthening community life among peasant farmers.

PROJECT: The work team carried out the project in two phases. In the first phase, they built the overall design on a single level and developed the priority elements: a multipurpose classroom and a toilet block, connected by a covered walkway. In the second phase, they added an open classroom for cultural events and a volume with a community kitchen, again connecting the spaces via the walkway. With this L-shaped circulation, they created an empty esplanade for communal events within the site and a built perimeter, following the traditional Quiané settlement pattern. The process incorporated local building systems using natural materials. In association with workers from the community, they made adobe bricks for the multipurpose classroom, bahareque (bamboo and earth) walls for the open classroom, permeable wooden lattices, and load-bearing structures in Oaxacan pine.

Students:

Phase One
K. Barón,
K. Bauer,
R. Caizergues,
M. Chiriboga,
A. Goncalves,
F. Hecht,
L. Holzapfel,
S. Kayser,
V. Kozma,
M. Kurz,
A. Matulla,
O. Petrenko,
D. Rader,
T. Reiner,
M. Rottenwaller,
P. Sauer,
P. Streit,
F. Stuffer,
M. Tichy,
J. Weise,
H. Wiesenfeld,
M. Yücesan,
Phase 2—A
M. Braun,
M. Chiriboga,
E. Eichinger,
M. Felber,
M. Fernández,
K. Franzl,
M. Gutmann,
M. Hartel,
A. Hoelzel,
D. Lins,
M. Mangas,
F. Menz,
E. Neubauer,
L. Ostermeier,
I. Pinto,
J. Schuldt,
M. Schwarz,
A. Sedlmeir,
L. Völkner,
La Salle
University Oaxaca
M. Alvarado,
R. Avendaño,
A. Cortés,
B. Gasga,
J. Morales,
P. Pérez,
R. Quintana,
I. Ramírez,
N. Reyes,
A. Rodríguez,
S. Villacaña.

In partnership with:

Munich
University
of Applied
Sciences—Ursula
Hartig, Jörg
Jungwirth,
Ferdinand
Loserth.
Communal, ejido,
and municipal
authorities of
Santa Catarina
Quiané. Center
for the Support
of the Oaxacan
Popular
Movement,
Campoac; Front
for the Defense
of the Earth.

Materials:

Cost:

Photography:
Paulina Ojeda.

Final Re- marks

FELIPE MESA

Design-build studios in Latin America have evident educational and curricular qualities for the teaching of architecture: collaboration rather than competition between students; teamwork together with changing responsibilities that draws on the individual skills of each participant; a greater balance with regard to architectural representation activities by permitting direct intervention in specific contexts; management of financial and material resources; building social relations; and group or dispersed authorship, among other educational elements. However, we often take it as a given that all of these properties are desirable in our teaching processes, while ignoring the architectural qualities of the projects built under these conditions.

Two questions arise: what are the dominant features of these architectural projects, and why is this architecture important today? The processes deployed in these courses lead to projects that are both necessary—required and desired—and lightweight; transformable and open; participatory rather than imposed. They are shaped by flexible and complementary geometries, by available materials, and by mixed technology, where almost nothing goes to waste. These methodologies are directed towards an architecture of contingent forms without clear styles, one that is small-scale, with great intensity of use and permeability. They lead to projects that express various facets of sustainability in architecture: the recycling and reuse of spaces and materials; implementation of bioclimatic strategies; and the use of local techniques, renewable resources, and strategies of social inclusion. In general, we can say they are naked, usable, and perform well in difficult conditions. This cluster of qualities, generated in the Latin American social and academic context, is of great importance, not only because it questions and complements large-scale, robust, and lasting public or institutional architecture by *auteurs* or well-known architects, but also because it responds in a sympathetic, inclusive, and forward-looking manner to the great twenty-first-century challenges of social inequality and environmental crisis.

Finally, the processes of these Latin American design-build studios differ from classic architectural studios with their extensive output of drawings, diagrams, and models; the stratified organization of firms and their commercial responsibilities and interests; and the experimental or research studios with their products aimed at publications, galleries, or specialist biennials. The methodologies and strategies they implement open up and support a new format for the production of architecture that is midway between academia and professional practice, one that strengthens the discipline and serves community interests.

FELIPE MESA is a founding partner of *Plan:b Arquitectos*, an architecture studio based in Medellín, Colombia—www.planbarq.com—and is Assistant Professor at The Design School—Architecture Program—of Arizona State University. In 2013 and 2018 he co-directed the Design-Build Studio *Nubes de Madera* at the School of Architecture of the Pontifical Bolivarian University, Medellín. Felipe Mesa conceives of the architectural project as a provisional pact, permeable configuration, and positive expression of the ecological and social forces around us. His projects and research into the practice and teaching of architecture have been published by *Mesaestándar* in four books: *Acuerdos Parciales* (2005), *Arquitectura en espera* (2007), *Permeabilidad* (2013), and *Arquitectura inversa* (2017); and the book *12 Projects in 10 Constraints* (2021), published by AR+D publishing.

ANA VALDERRAMA is co-founder of Matéricos Periféricos, a collective that works for social and environmental justice based in Rosario, Argentina. She is director of the Master's in Landscape Architecture and Associate Professor of the School of Architecture at the National University of Rosario. Ana Valderrama conceives of architecture as congealed emergences of a multiple and dialogical framework of human and non-human vitalities through time. She is currently completing a doctorate in Landscape Architecture at the University of Illinois. Her projects, works, and research have appeared in specialist journals and books, including *Poéticas colectivas*, published by Bisman Ediciones (2019).

GUSTAVO DIÉGUEZ forms part of the a77 architecture team based in Buenos Aires, Argentina, where he develops projects relating to auto-construction, the reuse of industrial waste and recycling applied to experimental housing, the creation of ephemeral institutions, the activation of social dynamics in the public space, and the self-management of cultural spaces. He is Associate Professor of the a77 Studio seminar in Architecture and Urban Design at the School of Architecture, Design and Urbanism of the University of Buenos Aires, and Professor at the Institute for Architecture and Urbanism of the National University of San Martín, Argentina.

Au-thors

IVÁN IVELIC YANES graduated as an architect from the Pontifical Catholic University of Valparaíso and holds a doctorate from the King Juan Carlos University of Madrid. He is currently Associate Professor at the School of Architecture and Design of the Pontifical Catholic University of Valparaíso, where he has worked continuously since 1995. A member and resident of the Open City of Amereida since 1970, he used this site as a base for contributing to the exploration of new forms of thinking about and developing architecture from an artistic and collective perspective. He has been a visiting professor in Argentina, Belgium, Switzerland, Spain, Germany, Greece, and New Zealand, where he has held conventions, workshops, conferences, exhibitions, and projects.

ANDRÉS GARCÉS ALZAMORA holds a doctorate in architecture from the Technical University of Catalunya-Barcelona, is a Professor at the School of Architecture and Design of the Pontifical Catholic University of Valparaíso, and a member of Amereida-Ciudad Abierta since 1994. His research focus is set out in his book *La ciudad teatro: El lugar de la escena y el otro lugar* (2019). He has undertaken twenty-five journeys with students across the American continent and created works of public and private architecture and urban design, as well as set designs for theater, opera, dance, and exhibitions, such as *Desvíos de la deriva* at the Museo Reina Sofía, Madrid, in 2010. He participated in the thirtieth Sao Paulo Art Biennial 2012 and Documenta 14 in Kassel and Athens (2017), representing the Amereida group.

DAVID BARRAGÁN, PASCUAL GANGOTENA, MARIALUISA BORJA, AND ESTEBAN BENAVIDES together make up the Al Borde architecture studio founded in 2007 and based in Quito, Ecuador. Their collaborative, multidisciplinary, and experimental work is characterized by their search for minimal solutions and projects that are stripped of everything that is superficial and extra, and notable for their raw materiality. Their academic engagement is an extension of the studio, and for this reason is also known as Al Borde Studio. They currently work as visiting professors at the University of Sciences and Arts of Latin America in Lima, Peru; and at the University of the Americas in Santiago, Chile. In 2020 Arquine published a monograph on their work under the title *Less Is All*, in reference to their quest for the essential. In 2019 they co-produced the documentary *Doing Much with Little,* which portrays the reality of a new generation of architects in Ecuador trained since the financial crisis of the year 2000.

Participants

MIGUEL MESA is a founding partner at Mesaestándar, a design studio and publishing house based in Medellín, Colombia. Between 2004 and 2021 he was professor in the Projects department of the School of Architecture of the Pontifical Bolivarian University, and in 2013 and 2018 he co-directed the Design-Build Studio *Nubes de Madera* at the same institution. In 2008 he published the book *La arquitectura del hueco*, based on his doctoral thesis. Miguel Mesa's work focuses on researching and producing content for the graphic design and publishing sector. In the past fifteen years he has designed and published more than 150 books in the fields of visual arts, architecture, and the city. His work can be seen at www.mesaestandar.com.

ALFONSO GARDUÑO is a founding partner at g3arquitectos, a studio that develops residential, cultural, commercial, and institutional projects in Mexico and the United States. He was Professor at the School of Architecture of the Monterrey Institute of Technology and Higher Education, Querétaro campus, between 1988 and 2015; and Program Director of the same institution between 2007 and 2011. Alfonso Garduño was Director of Strategic Projects at the Querétaro Municipal Mobility Secretariat between 2015 and 2018. His academic and professional work has been presented in a number of locations including Harvard GSD in 2007 and at the Quito Architecture Biennial 2014. The work of g3arquitectos has been recognized with a number of international prizes, including a nomination for the Mies Crown Hall Americas Prize 2016.

LUCAS GILARDI forms part of the architecture team at a77 based in Buenos Aires, Argentina, where he develops projects relating to auto-construction, the reuse of industrial waste and recycling applied to experimental housing, the creation of ephemeral institutions, the activation of social dynamics in the public space, and the self-management of cultural spaces. He is Associate Professor of the a77 Studio seminar in Architecture and Urban Design at the School of Architecture, Design and Urbanism of the University of Buenos Aires, and Professor at the Institute for Architecture and Urbanism of the National University of San Martín, Argentina.

ALEJANDRO HAIEK holds a Master's in Architectural Design from the Central University of Venezuela, and is a doctoral candidate at the University of Genoa, Italy. He is a founding partner of the studio Lab.Pro.Fab. where he participates in collaborative projects both professional and academic. Currently he is Lecturer Professor at the Umeå School of Architecture, in Sweden. His research is focused on collective landscapes, postindustrial ecologies, and network governance policies. His projects are developed at the intersection between design, arts, and social reengineering, incorporating both scientific advances and local traditions. The work of Lab.Pro.Fab has received multiple awards, including First Prize at the International Architecture Festival of Barcelona and the International Award for Public Art in Shanghai.

CARLOS HERNÁNDEZ CORREA graduated as an architect from the University of the Andes, is Associate Professor at the Pontifical Javeriana University in Bogotá, and Director of the International Experiences Program (PEI) at the same institution. His work focuses on the relationship between professional practice and the teaching of architecture. Carlos Hernández understands the studio as a laboratory that is useful for society, in which academic projects are built through participatory processes, applying the methodology of Collective Intelligences. His courses generate continuous reflection on architecture's ability to produce changes in vulnerable social and ecological contexts.

ANTONIO YEMAIL is an architect and industrial designer with a Master's degree in Construction. He has won distinctions at the Colombia, Quito, and Ibero-American Biennials. His work addresses different scales and formats with spatial solutions that prioritize the clarity of structure and simplicity of resources, through both the studio he founded in 2007—Yemail Arquitectura—and his teaching at the University of the Andes in Bogotá, Colombia, where he explores the relationship between ecological, material, and cultural diversity as a means of interpretation of contemporary culture. He is currently preparing his first monograph, *Cofres, alquimias y colisiones*, for the journal *Proa* (2022).

MARCELO BARRALE is co-founder of the Matéricos Periféricos collective and Associate Research Professor at the School of Architecture of the National University of Rosario, Argentina. Since 2001 he has led the academic research platform *Arquitectura de los bordes y la periferia*, monitoring and publishing essays about the works carried out in the peripheral areas of Rosario. Marcelo Barrale has extensive institutional experience, having been Outreach Secretary (1994–99) and Vice-Dean (2004–11) at the School of Architecture, Planning and Design of the Universidad de Rosario (FAPyD); publishing director of *Revista 041*; jury member for professional competitions for the College of Architects of the Provincia de Santa Fe; Secretary of the Argentine Federation of Architects' Associations (2000–02); and adviser to the Institute for Regional Development (IDR).

JOSÉ LUIS URIBE holds a doctorate in architecture from the Higher Technical School of Architecture of Madrid, Technical University of Madrid. His practice is focused on the dissemination of architecture culture, publishing the books *Talca, cuestión de educación* (2013), *Against the Tide* (2016), and *Viaje a Paraguay* (2022). He also directed the film *Feos, Sucios y Malos: Una Arquitectura Contemporánea en Latinoamérica* (2022). He was awarded the Premio IX BIAU (Argentina, 2014), the DAM Architectural Book Awards (Germany, 2014), and was curator of the Chilean Pavilion for the fifteenth International Architecture Exhibition of the Biennale di Venezia (2016). He is currently Professor at the School of Architecture of the University of Talca, Chile.

ALEJANDRO HERNÁN BORRACHIA is Dean of the Higher School of Architecture and Design at the University of Morón, Associate Professor of Architecture I and II, and Director of the Research Institute in Design and Georeferencing. He is seminar leader for the Final Project, in charge of the Federal Academic Support Program (PAAF), a thesis system undertaken at full scale in the school itself. Alejandro Borrachia is director of Estudio Borrachia Arquitectos, whose projects have won multiple national and international awards and are published in specialized media around the world. He is the author of the book *Nuevas arquitecturas en un mundo hiperconectado*, published by the University of Morón in 2015.

MARCELO STARICCO graduated as an architect and holds a Master's and doctorate from the School of Architecture, Design and Urbanism of the University of the Republic of Uruguay. He is Assistant Professor for architectural projects at Danza Studio. He has experience in the management and design of complex buildings: hospitals, clinics, laboratories, offices, educational buildings, etc. Since 2019 he has been founding partner at the firm Danza-Cotignola-Staricco, architects with whom he engages in professional practice focused on buildings on different scales, as well as intensive academic activity.

MARCELO DANZA is founding partner at the firm Danza-Cotignola-Staricco, specializing in hospital buildings. He is Dean of the School of Architecture, Design and Urbanism of the University of the Republic of Uruguay, and seminar leader for architectural and urban projects at the same university. He holds a Certificate of Research Proficiency from the Higher Technical School of Architecture of Madrid and is completing a doctorate in Architectural Projects at the FADU, UdelaR. He was a curator for the Uruguay Pavilion at the Architecture Biennale in Venice 2008 and 2016, and has been visiting professor and lecturer at a number of universities in the U.S. and Europe.

JUAN PABLO CORVALÁN HOCHBERGER graduated as an architect from the School of Engineers of Geneva, and the University of Chile. He holds a Master's in Architecture from the Berlage Institute Rotterdam, and is a doctoral candidate in Geography at the Pontifical Catholic University, Chile. He is a founding member of the international collective Supersudaca and the Susuka anti-office for projects, in Santiago, Chile. His work is focused on strengthening the multidisciplinary relationship with socio-spatial complexity, by means of a dialectic between academia and practice. Currently, he is Dean of the School of Architecture, Animation, Design and Construction at the University of the Americas in Chile.

JULIO SUÁREZ is co-founder of the República Portátil (2003), a Chilean collective that develops a critical spatial practice in public space. He is Professor at the School of Architecture of the University of the Americas in Chile, where he also leads the Master's in Socio-Spatial Practices. His most notable works include *Pabellón FAV* (2014), *Pabellón CCP* (2016), and *Antelia* (2019).

LEANDRO CAPPETTO is an architect whose work includes research and projects critical of neoliberalism. He is a founding member of the architecture collective TOMA, where he has engaged in a theoretical, performance-based, and speculative practice since 2012. He runs La Escuela Nunca and Otros Futuros, an independent architecture school; he is the co-founder and editor of FAN, a platform for publishing and debating architecture and culture. His career as a professor and researcher at universities in Argentina, Chile, and Australia has seen his work presented in different countries, while his theoretical, professional, and academic work has been published by a range of national and international media.

LUKAS FÚSTER works with Javier Corvalán on medium- and large-scale projects, generally connected with public use. He develops independent projects with design strategies that seek to obtain material resources by means of exchange, collection, self-management, and self-building. He was Professor of Architecture at the E Studio in the School of Architecture, Design, and Art of the National University of Asunción, Paraguay (2013–21); Professor of Technology at the School of Architecture of Talca, Chile (2021–22); and Professor WAVE at the IUAV, in Venice (2015, 2019, and 2020).

GUIDO MARTÍNEZ YAMBAY worked on the Architecture Laboratory with Javier Corvalán and Lukas Fúster developing projects and buildings. He began his independent practice in 2020, principally in the Metropolitan Area of Asunción, Paraguay. Currently he develops a range of projects that reuse different kinds of materials. He is Assistant Professor in the Studio Project seminar of the third semester of E Studio at the School of Architecture of the National University of Asunción, Paraguay.

SERGIO YBARRA is a student at the School of Architecture, Design, and Art in the National University of Asunción, Paraguay. He has worked on a number of social academic projects for the organization Aqua Alta. He is Assistant Professor in the Studio Project seminar of the third semester of E Studio at the School of Architecture of the National University of Asunción, Paraguay. His research is focused on the use of alternative materials for construction, in particular biodegradable materials.

LORENA BURBANO graduated as an architect from the University of Oregon in the U.S. and holds a postgraduate in Anthropology and Development Studies from KU Leuven, Belgium. She has always sought to support collectives and movements in their struggles for social justice. In 2016 she co-founded Atarraya, a studio focused on supporting collective processes of socio-spatial transformation out of practice, activism, and the academy. She is currently part of Mujeres de Frente, a feminist collective in her native Quito, which seeks to research the reproduction of urban life from a gender perspective.

SEBASTIÁN OVIEDO was born in Quito, Ecuador. His professional and academic work focuses on the forms of reproduction of habitat collectives and communities in Latin America. His work at Atarraya, the studio he founded in 2016, combines practice, research, activism, and teaching, and has won him a number of international awards. Sebastián Oviedo is an architect with postgraduate degrees in Human Settlements and Urbanism, Landscape and Planning from KU Leuven, Belgium. He currently works with the Kitu Kara people researching the interaction between indigenous territories and urbanization processes in Quito.

Adorno, Theodor W. *Teoría estética*. Translated by Jorge Navarro Pérez. Madrid: Ediciones Akal, 2004.

Bader, Simone et al., eds. *Experience in Action! DesignBuild in Architecture*. Munich: Detail, 2020.

Bennett, Jane. *Vibrant Matter: A Political Ecology of Things*. Durham: Duke University Press, 2010.

Berni, Antonio. Fundación Malba. Museo de Arte Latinoamericano de Buenos Aires. https://www.malba.org.ar/evento/antonio-berni-juanito-y-ramona/.

Boal, Augusto. *Teatro del oprimido*. Mexico City: Talleres Gráficos Continental, 1989.

Boal, Cecilia. "Critical 13/13. Critical theory texts. 13 seminars at Columbia." Accessed October 10, 2022. http://blogs.law.columbia.edu/critique1313/4-13/.

Bongman, Seo. "Borrowing Money. Aid, debt and dependence." In *A World of Difference. Encountering and Contesting Development*, edited by Eric Sheppard et al., 559–93. New York: Guilford Press, 2009.

Cardenal, Ernesto. *Los ovnis de oro: Poemas indios*. Mexico City: Siglo XXI, 1998.

Chu, Cecilia L. and Romola Sanyal. "Spectacular cities of our time." *Geoforum* 65 (2015), 399–402.

Colomina, Beatriz et al., eds. *Radical Pedagogies*. Cambridge, MA: MIT Press, 2022.

Comisión Sectorial de Investigación Científica, CSIC, de la Universidad de la República, Montevideo, Uruguay. "Reflexión en la Acción." *Folders 3*, vol. 03 (2022).

Cortázar, Julio. *From the Observatory*. Translated by Anne McLean. New York: Archipelago Books, 2011.

Cortázar, Julio, and Juan Fresán. *Casa tomada.* Buenos Aires: Ediciones Minotauro, 1969.

Cruz, Alberto. *El acto arquitectónico*. Valparaíso, Chile: Ediciones Universitarias de Valparaíso, 2010.

DeLanda, Manuel. "A Comparison of Deleuze's Assemblage Theory and the New Materialist Approach," lecture delivered at the Assemblage Thinking Symposium 2017, Department of Geography, University of the Aegean. Accessed October 10, 2022. http://www.youtube.com/watch?v=VzJq1OXUASA.

DeLanda, Manuel. *A New Philosophy of Society. Assemblage Theory And Social Complexity*. New York: Bloomsbury, 2016.

DeLanda, Manuel. *A Thousand Years of Nonlinear History*, edited by Jonathan Crary, Stanford Kwinter, and Bruce Mau. New York: Swerve Editions, 2000.

Deleuze, Gilles and Felix Guattari. *A Thousand Plateaus: Capitalism and Schizophrenia*. Translated by Brian Massumi. London: Continuum, 1998.

DeMichelis, Marco; Scimemi, Maddalen et al., eds. *EMBT Miralles Tagliabue: obras y proyectos*. Milán: Skira Editores, 2002.

Descola, Philippe. *Más allá de naturaleza y cultura*. Translated by Horacio Pons. Buenos Aires-Madrid: Amorrortu editores, 2012.

Elster, Jon. *Ulysses Unbound*. Cambridge: Cambridge University Press, 2000.

Escuela de Arquitectura UCV. *Amereida Travesías 1984 a 1988*. Valparaíso: Ediciones e[ad], 2011.

Falk, Richard. "Resisting 'Globalization-from-Above' Through 'Globalization-from-Below.'" In *Globalization and the Politics of Resistance. International Political Economy Series*, ed. Gills, B. K. London: Palgrave Macmillan, 2000.

Fernández-Galiano, Luis. *The Architect Is Present*. Madrid: Avisa/Museo ICO, 2014.

Focillon, Henri. *The Life of Forms in Art*. New York: Wittenborn, Shultz, 1948.

Forty, Adrian. *Primitivo. La palabra y el concepto*. Santiago, Chile: Ediciones ARQ. 2018.

Freear, Andrew et al. *Rural Studio at Twenty: Designing and Building in Hale County, Alabama.* New York: Princeton Architectural Press, 2014.

Freire, Paulo. *Pedagogía de la indignación: cartas pedagógicas en un mundo revuelto*. Buenos Aires, Argentina: Siglo Veintiuno editores, 2012.

Freire, Paulo. *Pedagogy of the Oppressed*. New York: Seabury Press, 1970.

Friedman, B. H., ed. *Give My Regards to Eighth Street: Collected Writings of Morton Feldman*. Cambridge, MA: Exact Change, 2000.

Harvey, David. *The 'New' Imperialism: Accumulation by Dispossession*. Oxford: Oxford University Press, 2003.

Hooks, Bell. "Theory as Liberatory Practice." *Yale JL & Feminism* 4 (1991).

Ingold, Tim. *Being Alive: Essays on Movement, Knowledge and Description*. New York: Routledge, 2011.

Ingold, Tim. "Materials Against Materiality." *Archaeological Dialogues* 14 (1) (2007), 1–16.

Ingold, Tim. "The Textility of Making." *Cambridge Journal of Economics* 34 (2010), 91–102.

Iommi M., Godofredo. *Carta del errante*. Valparaíso: Escuela de Arquitectura UCV, 1976.

Jennings, Michael W., Brigid Deherty, and Thomas Y. Levin, eds. *Walter Benjamin*: *The Work of Art in the Age of its Technological Reproducibility and Other Writings on Media*. Translated by Edmund Jephcott, Rodney Livingstone, Howard Eiland, et al. Cambridge, MA: Belknap Press of Harvard University Press, 2008.

Kafka, Franz. "The Cares of a Family Man." In *The Complete Stories*. Translated by Willa and Edwin Muir. London: Allen Lane, 1983.

Latour, Bruno. *Reassembling the Social: An Introduction to Actor-Network-Theory*. Oxford: Oxford University Press, 2005.

Lepik, Andrés and Barry Bergdoll. *Small Scale, Big Change: New Architectures of Social Engagement*. New York: Museum of Modern Art, 2010.

Lucretius. *On the Nature of the Universe*. Translated by Roland Latham. Baltimore: Penguin, 1961.

Max-Neef, Manfred. *U.S. Is Becoming an Underdeveloping Nation*, filmed September 2010. Accessed October 10, 2022. https://www.youtube.com/watch?v=hjcbBnM2OUo.

Mesa, Felipe and Miguel Mesa. *Nubes de madera*. Medellín: Mesaestándar, 2017.

Miraftab, Faranak. "Insurgent Practices and Decolonization of Future(s)." *The Routledge Handbook of Planning Theory*, edited by Michael Gunder, Ali Madanipour, and Vanessa Watson, 276–88. New York: Routledge, 2017.

Nancy, Jean-Luc. "Infinite History." In *The Birth to Presence*. Translated by Brian Holmes et al. Stanford: Stanford University Press, 1993.

Negri, Antonio. *De la fábrica a la metrópolis*. Buenos Aires: Editorial Cactus, 2020.

Ortiz, José Luis Uribe, ed. *Talca, Cuestión de educación*. Mexico City: Arquine, 2013.

Pallasmaa, Juhani. *The Thinking Hand*. Chichester: Wiley, 2009.

Portal, Fernando, ed. *Academia como práctica*. Santiago, Chile: Ediciones Academia Espacial, 2020.

Revista Matéricos Periféricos, issues 1 to 16. Accessed October 10, 2022. www.matericosweb.com.

Rocha, Glauber. "Aesthetics of Hunger," lecture delivered at the Latin American Cinema conference held in Genoa, Italy, 1965. In Michael Chanan, ed., *Twenty-Five Years of the New Latin American Cinema*. Translated by Burnes Hollyman and Randal Johnson. London: BFI, 1983.

Staricco, Marcelo, ed. *Placer en la Disciplina*. Montevideo: Producción de Taller Danza, Universidad de la República, 2016.

Stonorov, Tolya ed. *Design-Build Studio: Crafting Meaningful Work in Architecture Education.* New York: Routledge, 2018.

Sztulwark, Diego. *La ofensiva sensible. Neoliberalismo, populismo y el reverso de lo político.* Buenos Aires: Editorial Caja Negra, 2019.

Taller Danza. "Especies de Espacios." *Revista Mapeo*. Facultad de Arquitectura, Diseño y Urbanismo de la Universidad de la República Montevideo, Uruguay, vol. 15, (2016).

Uribe, José Luis. *Feos, sucios y malos: una mirada hacia la arquitectura latinoamericana contemporánea*, audiovisual work. Asunción, Paraguay: XI Bienal Internacional de Arquitectura y Urbanismo, 2019.

Valderrama, Ana, et al. *Poéticas Colectivas*. Buenos Aires: Bisman Ediciones, 2018.

Yurkiévich, Saúl. *La movediza modernidad.* Madrid: Santillana, 1996.

Talle-res de Diseño y Cons-truc-ción en Latino ameri-ca

ENSEÑANDO A TRAVÉS
DE UNA AGENDA SOCIAL

La búsqueda de lo real

FABRIZIO GALLANTI

Desde tiempos inmemoriales los arquitectos se han enfrentado a las dificultades de predecir el futuro a través del diseño. En lenguas romances, el término *diseño* es equivalente a las palabras *progetto, projet, proyecto*, del latín *projectus*, que significa *lanzar algo hacia adelante*, por lo tanto, prever activamente el futuro.

Un objeto tangible y real en el espacio —un edificio, para simplificar— se ejecuta después de realizar una secuencia compleja de acciones para imaginarlo, planear su construcción y, finalmente, construirlo. Las dos primeras fases, imaginar un edificio y trazar la secuencia de actividades que conducen a su ejecución, constituyen lo que convencionalmente se considera *diseño o proyecto*.

Numerosos investigadores han identificado en el Renacimiento italiano, con la construcción de la cúpula de la catedral de Florencia por Filippo Brunelleschi y los tratados de Leon Battista Alberti, el surgimiento de la figura moderna del arquitecto, diferenciada de los constructores. A través de dibujos e instrucciones, el arquitecto piensa en la construcción en términos abstractos y luego coordina a otros para que la ejecuten bajo su dirección. Durante siglos, la tensión entre el acto intelectual de imaginar un edificio y los tecnicismos de realmente *hacerlo* ha estado en el núcleo de la arquitectura. Los arquitectos aprendían su oficio trabajando en los talleres de maestros mentores, más tarde, estudiando en las academias de bellas artes. Solo a raíz de la industrialización y la aparición de una nueva figura profesional, el ingeniero, surgieron las escuelas de arquitectura a finales del siglo XIX en Europa y Estados Unidos. Incluso hoy, sus metodologías de enseñanza conectan estos dos linajes. Por un lado, en torno a la representación, derivada de la herencia de las bellas artes —pensemos en la *charrette*—. De otro lado, en torno a la construcción, derivada del legado de la ingeniería civil —pensemos en el cálculo, todavía un obstáculo aterrador para los estudiantes de primer año—.

Desde el reconocimiento de los protocolos educativos de la Bauhaus en la primera mitad del siglo XX, algunas dudas han seguido inquietando a muchos de los implicados en la enseñanza de la arquitectura. ¿Es posible aprender a construir solo en abstracto y solo dibujando? Una vez en la obra, ¿los arquitectos recién graduados sabrán cómo funcionan realmente *las cosas* solo porque han estudiado, redibujado e inventado detalles técnicos a escala 1:5 o 1:1? ¿Estarán preparados para discutir con ingenieros y contratistas?

En respuesta a tales dudas, la convicción de que el acto de construir solo puede ser *aprehendido haciendo*, ha llevado a un número creciente de escuelas de arquitectura en el mundo a ejecutar proyectos 1:1 construidos por estudiantes e incorporados dentro de sus planes de estudio. El sitio de construcción, colocado convencionalmente al final de la metodología del diseño arquitectónico, ha vuelto al núcleo del aprendizaje, aunque tenga el tamaño de un pabellón, sea una pequeña casa o la disposición de un espacio público definido. A su alrededor convergen los diferentes campos de especialización, se movilizan los materiales, con su peso y textura, y se compromete el trabajo físico. Además, aparece la figura fantasmal del *usuario*, ya que todos estos proyectos tienen uno o varios; en las versiones más básicas, los propios alumnos y profesores; en otros emprendimientos más ambiciosos, comunidades y habitantes reales, con sus deseos y necesidades.

Tal enfoque, visto por primera vez en numerosas escuelas inspiradas en la Bauhaus y continuado a través de las experimentaciones de instituciones alternativas como el *Black Mountain College* o la Pontificia Universidad Católica de Valparaíso entre 1960 y 1970, se ha establecido en contextos muy diversos. *Rural Studio* en la Universidad de Auburn en Alabama, el laboratorio ALICE en la EPFL en Lausana y la competencia *Solar Decathlon*, son solo algunos ejemplos de este creciente interés.

En el contexto latinoamericano, precursores como el *Taller de Diseño y Construcción, Travesías*, de la Pontificia Universidad Católica de Valparaíso o los proyectos de tesis de grado de la Universidad de Talca, ambos en Chile, han inspirado numerosas iniciativas que son objeto de esta publicación.

A lo largo de todos los casos de estudio del libro se identifican tres rasgos generales. La proximidad con la artesanía y los métodos de trabajo, todavía lejos de los sistemas altamente industrializados y prefabricados que se encuentran en Estados Unidos o el norte de Europa. La atención a una condición urbana donde extensas áreas son informales y autoconstruidas. Y, por último, la intención de brindar soluciones valiosas, en estrecha relación con las comunidades locales.

Los proyectos se vuelven reales no solo porque se construyen y ocupan una presencia tangible, sino porque están imbuidos de necesidades y deseos, rara vez son ejercicios académicos y formales. Son respuestas tácticas que aumentan la calidad de vida de las personas y generan formas híbridas novedosas de pensamiento arquitectónico, donde los procesos de retroalimentación en el intercambio con los usuarios y durante el proceso de construcción alteran de manera profunda y significativa la linealidad del proceso de diseño convencional, heredado de la mitología modernista. Este enfoque es esencialmente *aprender haciendo*, donde el aprendizaje no se limita a los años académicos, sino que se convierte en un enfoque constante que se aplica a cada proyecto futuro y permanece durante la carrera profesional.

Estos *Talleres de Diseño y Construcción* sugieren el surgimiento de un modelo nuevo y diferente para el arquitecto, quizás como un intelectual más práctico que está profundamente comprometido con los procesos de transformación y no solo los dirige desde arriba. Un arquitecto conocedor de la construcción, abierto a incorporar las habilidades de otros en sistemas de conocimiento y poder más horizontales. También podemos decir que —tal vez inconscientemente— esta búsqueda de lo *real* persigue un objetivo ambicioso y romántico de retroceder en el tiempo, volviendo a un momento idealizado, quizás en la Edad Media, cuando no había arquitectos como los conocemos hoy, sino maestros constructores.

Restricciones y acuerdos

FELIPE MESA

Esta publicación presenta el trabajo de catorce Talleres de Diseño y Construcción en Latinoamérica —México, Colombia, Venezuela, Ecuador, Paraguay, Chile, Argentina, Uruguay—. Reúne treinta y nueve construcciones de pequeño formato con programas sociales —salones, pabellones, plataformas, refugios, centros comunitarios, bibliotecas, comedores, escenarios, baños secos, pérgolas— en los que profesores, estudiantes, líderes comunitarios, representantes de municipios, organizaciones no gubernamentales y compañías privadas, trabajaron de manera colectiva. En la actualidad, estos espacios son mantenidos y usados por comunidades de estudiantes, campesinos, vecinos, pescadores, madres cabeza de familia o deportistas. A partir de los casos de estudio, el libro pone de manifiesto la idea de complejidad inherente al proceso de diseño y construcción en asocio con comunidades, renunciando a entenderla como un asunto únicamente formal.

La investigación asume las diversas restricciones en juego —inherentes, impuestas y autoimpuestas—[1], como fenómenos constructivos de la disciplina, con la habilidad de [...] nar situaciones positivas e inesperada[s] [...] como fuerzas externas que limitan la li[ber]tad creativa. Respalda con casos concre[tos] la idea de que los buenos edificios no tien[en que] ser necesariamente grandes, duraderos, ú[nicos], costosos, imponentes y de alta tecnolog[ía. Por] el contrario, agrupa pequeñas construc[ciones] efímeras, ordinarias, económicas y sutil[es que], con tecnologías mixtas, tienen un impacto [posi]tivo en sus comunidades. Propone que la [educa]ción de calidad en arquitectura no tiene [que ser] individual, elitista, aislada y competi[tiva], sino que puede ser comprometida social[mente], conectada al contexto y colaborativa. D[e esta] manera, *Talleres de Diseño y Construcc[ión en] Latinoamérica: Enseñando a través de una [agenda] social*, no solo ofrece posiciones nece[sarias] y estrategias urgentes en la educació[n y la] práctica contemporánea de la arquitectura [sino] también nuevas herramientas para acercar [nues]tra disciplina a la sociedad y sus crec[ientes] problemas, sin renunciar a la búsqueda re[flexi]va de nuevas cualidades estéticas.

Su carácter parcialmente bilingüe —in[glés y] español—, dirigido a un público de estudi[antes], arquitectos, diseñadores, artistas, activ[istas], entidades gubernamentales, y a un amplio g[rupo de] personas interesadas en las prácticas mate[riales] y el compromiso social, es la primera publi[cación] en reunir los principales Talleres de Di[seño y] Construcción en América Latina, con sus a[gendas] sociales y sus proyectos colaborativos.

En el contexto latinoamericano, esta [reco]pilación consolida de una manera colect[iva el] trabajo realizado en las últimas dos dé[cadas], revisando coincidencias, diferencias y [futu]ras oportunidades. Frente al resto del m[undo], el proyecto, con su énfasis en las restr[iccio]nes como fenómeno positivo, pretende a[mpliar] el conocimiento sobre los Talleres de D[iseño] y Construcción.

En el ámbito académico, esta edición pr[etende] impulsar la creación de nuevos talleres qu[e for]talezcan la enseñanza de la arquitectura a [través] de agendas sociales y la construcción de [edifi]cios o espacios con impactos concretos [en las] comunidades que los usan. En el ámbito pro[fesio]nal, ofrece un conjunto de valores, cuali[dades y] proyectos que quieren sacudir la forma de [pensar] de los arquitectos y, por lo tanto, sus prá[cticas] cotidianas. En el campo de las organiza[ciones] independientes y gubernamentales, el libr[o fun]ciona como un catálogo de opciones y estra[tegias] para impulsar nuevos proyectos en benefi[cio de] estudiantes y comunidades específicas.

Aunque los catorce casos de estudio qu[e pre]sentamos realizan diversos tipos de alian[zas con] municipios, organizaciones no gubernamen[tales] empresas privadas o comunidades independientes, el libro reúne, a grandes rasgos, dos tipos de Talleres de Diseño y Construcción. De un lado, los que forman parte fundamental y a largo plazo de alguna estructura curricular universitaria —Taller Travesías, Taller de Titulación de Talca, Taller Matéricos Periféricos, Taller PAAF, Taller Danza, Taller E, Taller de Intervención Comunitaria, Taller PEI—. Y de otro lado, los que hicieron parte de alguna estructura académica de manera temporal, desaparecieron o que han variado para adaptarse a los cambios institucionales, buscando mayor estabilidad —Taller Nubes de Madera, Taller Lab.Pro.Fab, Taller Al Borde, Taller Atarraya, Taller A77, Taller Activo—. Algunos casos como los talleres A77, Al Borde, o Lab.Pro.Fab, surgieron y se mantienen como prácticas profesionales estrechamente ligadas al trabajo social y a la educación de la arquitectura por medio de cursos ya consolidados en diversas universidades.

En todos los casos de estudio presentados, el diseño arquitectónico fue realizado por un grupo de profesores y estudiantes en alianza con comunidades y asesores técnicos. Los casos cuentan con tres modalidades de construcción. En la primera, algunos talleres poseen las condiciones institucionales para que sus estudiantes construyan con sus manos —diversos tipos de seguros—, dejando pocos procesos a obreros expertos. En la segunda modalidad, se establecen alianzas con empresas constructoras que asumen las responsabilidades legales, permitiendo a los estudiantes formar parte de un equipo de construcción liderado por expertos. Y, en la tercera, los cursos ceden la mayor parte de la responsabilidad constructiva a empresas aliadas y expertas que asumen la responsabilidad civil, permitiendo que los estudiantes se concentren en la supervisión de la obra, y en procesos de construcción menores, realizados en los talleres de construcción universitarios.

En la mayoría de los casos, todo el proceso de gestión, diseño y construcción, tarda un cuatrimestre académico siguiendo una línea de trabajo similar: un mes para definiciones generales, dos meses para diseñar, detallar, gestionar recursos y permisos, y un mes para construir. En ciertos casos los tiempos se expanden, los cursos utilizan uno o dos cuatrimestres académicos para la gestión y el diseño, y uno más para la construcción. Algunos cursos están diseñados para estudiantes de primer año —resulta importante aclarar que la carrera de arquitectura en Latinoamérica implica cursar cinco años o diez cuatrimestres académicos antes de obtener el título—, poniéndolos en contacto inmediato con comunidades, materiales y construcción. Otros, reciben estudiantes

de tercero y cuarto año, y promueven la interacción de estudiantes con diferentes experiencias para enfrentar los retos del proceso. Finalmente, algunas universidades dejan estos cursos para el último año y les otorgan mayor autonomía a los estudiantes en su desempeño. En todo caso, durante estos talleres los estudiantes construyen casi siempre su primer proyecto antes de graduarse.

Lo propio de los Talleres de Diseño y Construcción en Latinoamérica es su esfuerzo por generar simultáneamente una educación de calidad y un impacto concreto en comunidades vulnerables o con necesidades específicas. Para ello, y sin renunciar al interés por asuntos disciplinares, profesores y estudiantes diseñan estrategias de participación —reuniones, conversaciones, viajes, travesías, visitas, mesas redondas, talleres participativos, entrevistas, encuestas—, para definir localizaciones, programas, materiales, sistemas constructivos y mantenimiento futuro. Además, consumen gran cantidad de energía en la búsqueda de recursos económicos, implementando un amplio abanico de estrategias mezcladas: apoyo institucional de universidades, rifas, eventos estudiantiles, apoyo de familiares, municipalidades y empresas privadas, becas, donaciones locales o extranjeras y campañas en internet. En algunos casos los profesores proponen a los estudiantes reducir al mínimo la producción de representaciones —maquetas e impresiones—, para usar el dinero disponible en la construcción final. Ningún curso es igual a otro, pero todos mezclan en dosis diferentes los mismos componentes que permiten construir en muy poco tiempo intervenciones de pequeño formato en las que restricciones y acuerdos dan forma a la arquitectura.

El Taller de Diseño y Construcción de Valparaíso[2] —identificado en esta publicación como el Taller Travesías—, es el único taller originado a mediados del siglo pasado. Debido a su tradición y énfasis en el viaje, las travesías e intervenciones provisionales y poéticas en el paisaje rural, tuvo una importante influencia en los Talleres de Diseño y Construcción latinoamericanos, ya sea de manera directa o indirecta. El interés actual por este tipo de talleres en Latinoamérica, no solo obedece al renovado acento en una educación de la arquitectura cercana a la gente, los materiales y la construcción, sino, también, a los cambios políticos ocurridos a finales del siglo XX y principios del XXI, en los que en países como Argentina, Brasil, Uruguay, Venezuela, Colombia y Chile, gobiernos neoliberales, dieron paso a gobiernos de corte social-demócrata con un mayor interés por reducir la inequidad endémica de la región. La respuesta a estas situaciones políticas y educativas asume matices diversos en cada uno de los casos que presentamos; en términos generales, algunos gestionan lazos con comunidades urbanas, construyen infraestructura pública de pequeño formato y activan espacios subutilizados —Taller Matéricos Periféricos, Taller A77, Taller Danza, Taller E, Taller Lab. Pro.Fab, Taller de Intervención Comunitaria, Taller Activo—. Otros, en alianza con comunidades rurales, realizan intervenciones de pequeño formato, mezclando intereses ecosociales —Taller Nubes de Madera, Taller de Titulación de Talca, Taller Al Borde, Taller PAAF, Taller PEI, Taller Atarraya, Taller Travesías—.

Publicaciones realizadas por algunos de los talleres mencionados, evidencian sus apuestas académicas de manera integral. La Escuela de Arquitectura y Diseño de la Pontificia Universidad Católica de Valparaíso, publicó el libro *Amereida*[3]; la Escuela de Arquitectura de Talca, publicó el libro *Talca, cuestión de educación*[4]; el Taller Matéricos Periféricos de la Universidad de Rosario, publicó el libro *Poéticas Colectivas*[5]; el Taller Nubes de Madera, de la Facultad de Arquitectura de la Universidad Pontifica Bolivariana de Medellín, publicó el libro *Nubes de Madera*[6]; y, el Núcleo de Lenguaje y Creación de la Facultad de Arquitectura, Diseño y Construcción UDLA de Chile y su Taller de Intervención Comunitaria, publicó el libro *Academia como Práctica.*[7]

Aunque estos talleres Latinoamericanos se han desarrollado de manera independiente y aislada, es importante mencionar algunas referencias globales que, sin duda, han sido relevantes. Tal vez el caso más influyente para el contexto latinoamericano es el Rural Studio[8] de Auburn University en Estados Unidos, ampliamente difundido y con un trabajo sostenido durante las últimas tres décadas. Este Taller de Diseño y Construcción, fundado en 1993 por Samuel Mockbee (1944-2001) y D.K. Ruth (1944-2009), y hoy dirigido por Andrew Freear, hace énfasis en la educación de estudiantes de arquitectura a través del diseño y la construcción de edificios e intervenciones de pequeño formato —vivienda, infraestructura y espacios públicos— con gran impacto positivo en la vida cotidiana de comunidades rurales y vulnerables en Hale County, Alabama.

Es también importante resaltar que en el contexto de Estados Unidos y Europa se presenta una tradición consolidada de Talleres de Diseño y Construcción, evidente en dos publicaciones recientes. De un lado, el libro *Design-Build Studio, crafting meaningfull work in architecture education*[9], editado por Tolya Stonorov y publicado en 2018, reúne artículos y casos de estudio vinculados a universidades americanas y europeas. De otro lado, el libro *Experience in Action, DesignBuild in Architecture*[10], editado por Vera Simon Bader y Andres Lepik, y publicado como parte de una exhibición con el mismo nombre, reúne artículos, ensayos, entrevistas y 16 casos de estudio con proyectos en Europa, Estados Unidos y otros lugares del mundo. En esta última publicación, aunque todas las universidades son de Estados Unidos y Europa —a excepción del caso de la Universidad de [...]ón en Argentina—, en algunas ocasiones traba[jaron] en países del hemisferio sur como Cam[boya], Argentina, India, Sur África y Camerún. Ambas publicaciones desarrollan un trabajo pa[ralelo] al que presentamos en este libro, y refle[jan el] reciente interés por este modelo educa[tivo y] participativo en el contexto global.

De manera general, podemos decir q[ue los] talleres de diseño y construcción estadou[niden]ses, europeos y latinoamericanos, poseen [carac]terísticas similares, aunque los dos pr[imeros] exploran con mayor intensidad algunas i[nnova]ciones técnicas —métodos constructivos, [mate]riales, impresiones 3D, por nombrar algun[os—, y] los últimos exploran con mayor vigor algun[as in]novaciones sociales —métodos de particip[ación], estrategias de escucha e inclusión, gest[ión de] recursos económicos, entre otros—, dete[rmina]das siempre por contextos altamente rest[ricti]vos que obligan al uso de técnicas constru[ctivas] locales o mixtas.

Este libro no solo posee una estruct[ura de] capítulos independientes que permite co[mparar] y cruzar información de un caso con otro[, sino] también, permite una lectura homogénea y [unita]ria, agrupando el trabajo diverso en un so[lo es]fuerzo colectivo. Inicialmente, tres art[ículos] exploran el tema desde ángulos diferent[es: el] papel político de estos talleres, lo que [implica] aprender el mundo de ellos y, una de sus [estra]tegias principales, la escucha. A continu[ación,] el texto presenta los catorce casos de e[studio] con sus apuestas académicas y sociales, p[un]tos relevantes de cada uno y un mosaico [de fo]tografías de sus procesos. Por último, el [libro] ofrece un comentario final, concentrado [en las] cualidades pedagógicas y disciplinares d[e esta] arquitectura, en donde el énfasis social [y las] cualidades tectónicas particulares.

1. Jon Elster, *Ulises Unbound* (Cambridge: Cambri[dge] University Press, 2000), 190-221.
2. Beatriz Colomina et al. editores. *Radical Peda[gogies]* (Cambridge, MA: The MIT Press, 2022), 154-159.
3. *Amereida: travesías 1984 a 1988* (Valparaíso: Ediciones e[ad], 2011).
4. José Luis Uribe Ortiz, ed. *Talca, Cuestión de educación* (México D.F.: Arquine S.A de C.V, 2013).
5. Ana Valderrama et. al. *Poéticas Colectivas* (Bu[enos] Aires: Bisman Ediciones, 2018).

6. Felipe Mesa y Miguel Mesa. *Nubes de Madera* (Medellí: Mesaestándar, 2017).
7. Fernando Portal, ed. *Academia como Práctica* (Santiago de Chile: Ediciones Academia Espacial, 2020).
8. Andrew Freear et al. *Rural Studio at Twenty. Designing and Building in Hale County, Alabama* (New York: Princeton Architectural Press, 2014).
9. Tolia Stonorov, ed. *Design-Build Studio. Crafting Meaningful Work in Architecture Educatio.* (New York: Routledge, 2018).
10. Simone Bader et al., eds. *Experience in Action! DesignBuild in Architecture* (Munich: DETAIL, 2020).

Los Talleres de Diseño y Construcción: Entramados y decolonialidad

ANA VALDERRAMA

Cuando nuestra experiencia vivida de teorizar está fundamentalmente ligada a procesos de autorrecuperación, de liberación colectiva, no existe brecha entre la teoría y la práctica.[1]

En este ensayo me propongo contribuir al debate sobre las teorías y las prácticas decoloniales del *Sur global*, explorando las correlaciones entre los procesos y los productos de los Talleres de Diseño y Construcción y las dinámicas socio-políticas en las que se ven entramados. Los Talleres de Diseño y Construcción podrían entenderse como parte de las muchas experiencias de pedagogías basadas en la tierra o situadas. Las metodologías decoloniales situadas —indígenas, feministas, *queer*, entre otras—, han hecho y están haciendo un gran aporte en resistir los procesos de despojo a partir de desplegar experiencias *in situ, in vivo*, que reconectan el cuerpo con la tierra, porque son las tierras y los cuerpos los principales territorios de disputa del capitalismo actual. Entendiendo la tierra como un ente integral que incluye cielos, aguas, humanos y no humanos, estas metodologías proponen prácticas situadas integrales, colectivas y dialógicas capaces de articular saberes diversos e inter, trans o infraagencias.

Me interesa entonces exponer el potencial de los Talleres de Diseño y Construcción más allá de sus agendas pedagógicas regulares. Es decir, su capacidad para contrarrestar los procesos de inoculación de dispositivos de alienación y de despojo y para disolver las dicotomías modernas que impiden la comprensión de fenómenos complejos. Me posiciono inevitablemente desde mi condición de mujer latinoamericana, feminista, activista y cofundadora del colectivo Matéricos Periféricos[2], un grupo de arquitectos con base en Rosario, Argentina.

Matéricos Periféricos surgió durante la gran crisis financiera e institucional de la Argentina en 2001 y constituyó un colectivo de profesores universitarios, profesionales de la arquitectura y estudiantes, dedicados a coconstruir equipamientos e infraestructuras con comunidades en emergencia socioambiental a través de Talleres de Diseño y Construcción. Los talleres, a su vez, funcionan como dispositivos para reforzar los lazos sociales dentro de las comunidades vulneradas y para acompañar organizaciones de base y barriales en la resistencia a los dispositivos de poder real.

El ensayo propone una reflexión epistemológica y ontológica, es decir, tanto sobre la posicionalidad y direccionalidad político-cultural y disciplinar de nuestras prácticas desde la centralidad de la periferia, como sobre el ser de los artefactos, sus procesos de materialización y su forma como expresión de una resistencia a los procesos de despojo que se dan en esas periferias. Estas prácticas deben ser reexploradas y teorizadas, ya que las políticas públicas y la literatura sobre el diseño —en todas las escalas— «para» los desposeídos, frecuentemente han seguido las prescripciones del aparato político y disciplinario colonizador para penetrar en las comunidades y desmovilizar la resistencia. Es decir, sus reflexiones y acciones se han basado frecuentemente en la fetichización y mercantilización de los instrumentos de la resistencia convirtiéndolos en clientelismo o caridad —lo que ha llevado a soluciones empaquetadas e idealizadas que no han tenido en cuenta la comunidad local, los materiales, el flujo de energía y las culturas— o en una mirada romántica/conformista de la informalidad que ha reproducido las formas y expresiones de la pobreza, impidiendo que surjan otros sueños. En este sentido, la revisión de nuestras prácticas apoyada en ciertas especulaciones teóricas sobre el mundo socio-material podría permitirnos pergeñar ideas antes inimaginables y con ello interpretar, cuestionar y conferir nuevos significados a nuestras prácticas. En última instancia, como sugiere Bell Hooks, la especulación teórica es también una práctica emancipadora.[3]

CASA TOMADA

La conciencia del mundo, que hace posible mi conciencia, hace imposible la inmutabilidad del mundo.[4]

Las periferias del *Sur global* son los territorios en los que los dispositivos de *acumulación por desposesión*[5] se exponen obscenamente en el extremo del espectáculo, materializando todas las ironías de Debord. Cecilia Chu y Romola Sanyal[6] afirman que la proclamación de Guy Debord en 1967 sobre el espectáculo como principio de las sociedades modernas ha triunfado en las últimas décadas con la globalización capitalista neoliberal y la mercantilización del entorno construido. Las comunidades no representadas en el *Sur global* han sido, de hecho, una variable constante para la supervivencia del capitalismo. Es decir, la exclusión sistemática de los pobres hacia las periferias ha generado mano de obra barata y fácil acumulación de capital, mientras la gente es empujada cada vez más hacia campos marginales, tierras inhóspitas, lugares sin infraestructura, zonas inundables, sitios sin urbanizar.

Luego de la Segunda Guerra Mundial, este proceso de desplazamiento, estigmatización y despojo se aceleró con la ayuda de los organismos internacionales de crédito, la descentralización global, las divisiones del trabajo —raza, género, clase, espacio, tiempo—, y la separación entre poder económico y administración política local. Desde entonces hasta ahora, la capacidad metamórfica del capitalismo ha mercantilizado todo lo que encuentra a su paso —incluso iniciativas solidarias, estrategias participativas, ONG—, y el entramado socio-espacial de las ciudades ha sido la principal plataforma de flujo de capitales, generando una mayor inestabilidad social y falta de equidad.

Hoy en día, las fuerzas del capitalismo están totalmente desvinculadas de la geografía, las leyes, las instituciones y los gobiernos, y se caracterizan por procesos codiciosos y especulativos que toman la forma de agotamiento de la naturaleza y de fabricación sistemática de inestabilidad social, económica y ecológica, inequidad e injusticia. A lo largo de este proceso, los urbanistas han perdido por completo el objetivo original de reducir la brecha entre ricos y pobres respecto al derecho a la ciudad, como proclamó el urbanismo moderno durante el siglo XX. Por el contrario, la planificación ha sido solo una herramienta para legitimar la especulación inmobiliaria y las prescripciones de los organismos internacionales para desmovilizar y debilitar las prácticas de resistencia. En la mayoría de los casos, los profesionales han funcionado para prestigiar el clientelismo y la caridad de los funcionarios locales, o para elaborar publicaciones de planes políticamente correctos que nunca se materializarán. Las periferias del *Sur global* son como el cuento de Julio Cortázar *Casa tomada*[7] en el que una bestia omnipresente e invisible obliga a los pe[rsona]jes a retroceder de una habitación a ot[ra. Al] final del cuento, los personajes se esca[pan de] la casa y tiran las llaves a una alcanta[rilla.] ¿Podemos cambiar el final del relato?

CORRELACIÓN DE FUERZAS

> [...] cuando hay estrellas, hay anguila[s que] nacen en las profundidades atlánticas [y] empiezan, porque de alguna manera hay [que] empezar a seguirlas, a crecer, [...] bo[cas] que resbalan en una succión intermina[ble,] [...] ascenderán, leviatán, surgirá kra[ken] inofensivo y pavoroso para iniciar la migración a ras de océano [...][8]

Las prácticas colectivas de diseño deco[lonial] se despliegan entre los resquicios y super[posi]ciones de procesos jerárquicos —arriba-[abajo] y autoorganizados o en malla —abajo-arr[iba al] costado— que interactúan y cambian con el [tiempo] dando lugar a los procesos de formación y [trans]formación de los ambientes construidos. [Jerar]quías y mallas conviven, se entremezcla[n y] dan lugar unas a otras. Manuel DeLanda[9] en[tiende] estos procesos de formación y transforma[ción de] modo ontológico. Para él, los ambientes [urba]nos serían un emergente de flujos de mat[eria y] energía que se inician con procesos aut[oorga]nizados, pero una vez estabilizados en un[a for]ma, son capturados por las fuerzas jerár[quicas] que crean restricciones que las intens[ifican] o impiden su crecimiento a través de f[uerzas] de homogeneización y centralización. Es [decir,] los ambientes urbanos comienzan como em[ergen]tes de una ecología de instituciones —esc[uelas,] universidades, mercados—que toman deci[siones] colectivas. Sin embargo, una vez que al[canzan] estabilidad, son centralizadas por la bu[rocra]cia gubernamental que utiliza esas estru[cturas] para dominar y homogeneizar la sociedad q[ue le] dio forma. Deleuze y Guattari[10], por su [parte,] entienden la dinámica entre fuerzas jerár[quicas] y autoorganizadas como una doble articul[ación,] como pinzas de langosta que coexisten. Il[ustran] este concepto a través de la *máquina de ro[stros.]* Una *máquina de rostros* que tiene dos fa[ces:] *paredes blancas y agujeros negros*. Las *p[aredes] blancas* representan la producción coloni[al/capital]del rostro, el capitalismo, las fuerzas [jerár]quicas, los estratos, el espacio estriad[o, las] líneas de segmentación —que codifican y [terri]torializan—. Los *agujeros negros* represe[ntan la] producción social del rostro, la insurg[encia,] las *máquinas de guerra*, las fuerzas autoor[gani]zadas, el *cuerpo sin órganos*, el espacio [liso y] las líneas de fuga —que decodifican y des[terri]torializan para producir el devenir—.

INSURGENCIA

Nezahualcoyotl un día dijo:
Las dos principales materias de la
educación universitaria:
Ixlamachiliztli —dar sabiduría a los
rostros—
Yolmelahualiztli —fortalecer los corazones—
[…]
El Ministerio de Poesía
Abierto todo el día. El de Guerra
casi siempre cerrado. [11]

Las prácticas colectivas de diseño decolonial intentan contraponer un proyecto alternativo a partir de una participación activa en las correlaciones de fuerza que permita penetrar entre las grietas del proyecto totalizante, hegemónico y desigual de las ciudades. Cecilia L. Chu y Romola Sanyal afirman que

el capitalismo nunca puede reducirse a lógicas puras de acumulación de capital, y que la metrópoli moderna no es solo un escenario de dominación sino también de contestación y luchas políticas que siempre conlleva el potencial para el cambio revolucionario.»[12]

Richard Falks[13], por su parte, propone un movimiento de resistencia que llama *globalización desde abajo* que consiste en contrarrestar la globalización desde arriba desde el fortalecimiento de las identidades locales. Manfred Max-Neef[14] también destaca el valor de defender y proteger las identidades como modo de resistencia. El autor insiste en describir los valores y principios de comunidades no representadas en Chile que surgieron de las cenizas del capitalismo y resistieron la cultura de la codicia: solidaridad, creatividad, redes de cooperación, ayuda mutua. Seo Bongman[15], es mucho más pesimista; para él, el sistema globalizado ha incrementado sistemáticamente la pobreza, la destrucción de las industrias nacionales, la inestabilidad de las finanzas a través del endeudamiento internacional con el fantasma del llamado *desarrollo* y descarta cualquier posibilidad de reconciliación entre el *Sur global* y el sistema globalizado. Entre el optimismo de la resistencia y el pesimismo de la no reconciliación, ¿cuáles serían las posibilidades, los modos de operar de las prácticas de diseño decoloniales en el *Sur global*? En *Prácticas insurgentes y descolonización del futuro(s)*, Faranak Miraftab[16] propone la insurgencia como salida y define dos tipos de espacios insurgentes, invitados e inventivos. Los espacios invitados están definidos por acciones de base a través de

grupos informales comunitarios en alianza con gobiernos y otras instituciones. Los espacios inventivos, son acciones colectivas de los sectores populares que confrontan directamente a las autoridades y desafían y desestabilizan el *statu quo*. Las prácticas insurgentes definidas por Miraftab transitan entre ambos espacios, invitados e inventivos, ya que deben ser fluidos y moverse más rápido que el capitalismo. Sus acciones son a veces pacíficas, a veces violentas, fuera de la ley establecida o dentro de la ley. Son acciones que abordan la transgresión, la contrahegemonía y la imaginación para hacer emerger otro mundo radicalmente diferente.

FRAGMENTOS, COEXISTENCIAS, MULTIPLICIDADES

El *collage* es así la técnica más adecuada para manifestar la disparidad hirviente de nuestras realidades: la coexistencia de desigualdades flagrantes, antagonismos contemporáneos, contrastes explosivos. El *collage* es la combinación que permite simbolizar activamente la multiplicidad móvil y heterogénea de la realidad. [17]

Se presentan entonces dos preguntas primordiales: ¿Cómo podrían nuestros Talleres de Diseño y Construcción, en sus procesos y materializaciones, predecir una estética emergente de la sociedad y jugar un papel en un proyecto de emancipación tanto de la sociedad como de la propia disciplina? ¿Cuál sería la estrategia de los Talleres de Diseño y Construcción para penetrar entre las grietas del proyecto hegemónico? Walter Benjamin diría «…por primera vez en la historia mundial, la reproductibilidad técnica emancipa la obra de arte de su servidumbre parasitaria al ritual […] En lugar de estar fundada en el ritual, se basa en una práctica diferente: la política». [18]

Benjamin afirmaba que la aparición de los medios técnicos de producción y reproducción había producido una desacralización del arte o puesto en crisis el aura del arte.[19] Algo similar a lo que Adorno llamó la «crisis de la apariencia estética de la totalidad»,[20] aunque para él no se trataba de un producto de los medios de reproducción técnica sino de una respuesta a las condiciones históricas de la realidad que consideraba contradictorias y ya no accesibles a nuestra racionalidad. Benjamin estaba interesado en explorar la intersección entre el arte, la revolución, los modos de producción —en particular, la reproducción de obras de arte y el arte del cine— los procesos sensoriales y cognitivos humanos. El arte revolucionario para Benjamin era aquel capaz de encontrar fracturas del sistema desde dónde provocar la ruptura del sentido de continuidad de la cultura dominante. La estrategia se llevaría adelante por medio de múltiples acciones, de constelaciones. Las constelaciones podrían proporcionar mundos alternativos capaces de aumentar las correlaciones de fuerzas. Benjamin pensaba que el cine era un ejemplo de cómo las figuras del pensamiento o las imágenes dialécticas podían generar significados que de otro modo serían inaccesibles o irrepresentables. Las películas eran montajes de fragmentos o constelaciones que provocaban una reacción y daban acceso a nuevos mundos posibles.[21] La cámara introducía un movimiento dialéctico de distracción-choque que convertía la obra de arte en un arma a la vez que un *entrenamiento* para que el espectador aprendiera a mirar la realidad de otras formas. «El cine ha liberado el efecto de choque físico —que el dadaísmo había mantenido envuelto, por así decirlo, dentro del efecto de choque moral— de este envoltorio».[22]

Posteriormente, en 1980, Gilles Deleuze y Felix Guattari[23] ofrecieron una alternativa a la totalidad del capitalismo por medio de la esquizofrenia[24] y propusieron el *rizoma* como modelo, tanto para ofrecer medios de confrontación de las culturas hegemónicas dominantes, como para operar en el mundo socio-material. El rizoma era una multiplicidad que emergía de procesos no jerárquicos de autoorganización. Era un entramado heterogéneo que confrontaba totalidades hegelianas y concepciones arborescentes. Sus *agencements*[25] fueron concebidos como multiplicidades de agencias o conexiones y relaciones de contenidos y expresiones dentro de un mundo socio-material. Estas agencias podían materializarse en *estratos*, *ensamblajes* o *cuerpos sin órganos* según la intensidad de la territorialización y codificación de los componentes. Manuel DeLanda sintetizó posteriormente la ontología del *ensamblaje* de Deleuze y Guattari como una multiplicidad

> que tiene propiedades propias, no reducibles a las partes que también mantienen su autonomía. Las partes ejercen ciertas capacidades cuando interactúan entre sí, pero pueden separarse del *ensamblaje* en cualquier momento. La identidad del *ensamblaje* en cualquier punto del espacio y del tiempo estará determinada por un conjunto de parámetros e intensidades de territorialización y codificación.[26]

ENSAYOS EN VEZ DE ESPECTÁCULOS

> La poesía debe ser hecha por todos. Y no para uno [...] La poesía en acción emerge y se inserta en la realidad. Revela la posibilidad que funda toda existencia efectiva y al mismo tiempo se hace act... el mundo. He visto entonces al poeta s... de la literatura, sobrepasar el poema... incluso abandonar la escritura.[27]

Theodore Adorno y Walter Benjamin aseg... que después de Auschwitz el mundo había p... todo rasgo de humanidad y se había vuelto... prensible a nuestros ojos. Se preguntaba... sería el papel del arte en este mundo inco... sible e inhumano, cómo el arte podría expre... su forma, en su imagen, en su materialidad,... procesos de producción esa realidad inh... Benjamin estaba interesado en la potenci... del cine como forma de resistencia, sobr... en el modo en que esta disciplina prop... procesos participativos y se apropiaba... medios de producción actuales. Benjamin en... el cine como una *performance* producida y re... cida a través de un proceso participativo m... por la tecnología. Según él, en las pelícu... espectador se incorporaba al proceso de p... ción participando desde el punto de vista... de la cámara. De esta manera, el espectad... también crítico y completaba la obra de ar...

Benjamin pensaba en la obra de arte c... arma o como un *entrenamiento* para que... pectador aprenda a mirar la realidad de... maneras. Theodore Adorno, por su parte, p... que el arte no debía transformar el mundo... transformarse a sí mismo para expresar,... en evidencia la incomprensibilidad del... No había para él una directa relación en... reflexión del arte y la praxis de la revol... En ese sentido, Adorno se interesó en el... *del absurdo*, el de Becket y el de Ione... particular. Ese teatro absurdo era el... que expresaba el sinsentido del mundo de... desmantelamiento desde el interior de la... disciplina, deconstruyendo el sentido de... logo, las relaciones entre mensaje y pal... los procedimientos habituales, la prete... de forma final de la escena del teatro. De... mirada latinoamericana, Augusto Boal h... aporte similar recogiendo las experienci... *Teatro de Arena* y las formulaciones de F... Pero Boal pensaba que el arte sí podía... dispositivo de transformación social,... podía haber una relación entre arte y revo... y escribió un libro llamado *Poéticas polí*... que fue luego llamado *Teatro del oprimi*... diferencia de las películas de Benjamin,... *Teatro del oprimido* de Boal el espectador... legaba en el actor profesional el poder de... o actuar en su lugar. Los espectadores a... la representación, desmantelaban su prop... tructura corporal y mental, modificaban... ción teatral, ensayaban soluciones y de...

evoluciones de la escena. Es decir, se entrenaban en la acción teatral propiamente dicha. En este caso, podría ser que el teatro no fuera revolucionario en sí mismo, sino un entrenamiento para la revolución. El teatro era un movimiento desde la realidad hacia la idealidad —y no al revés— y era considerado para Boal, la semilla del cambio revolucionario. Augusto Boal decía que el teatro debe hacer caer los muros impuestos por las clases dominantes: todos debían actuar, todos debían participar activamente en las transformaciones. Boal lo llamó *sistema comodín* que significaba «la conquista de los medios de producción teatral»[31] por parte de los oprimidos. Entonces, el papel del teatro era activar la conciencia de la propia realidad, de las fuerzas estructurales de opresión e imaginar estrategias de emancipación. El teatro de Boal era un teatro-ensayo, no un teatro-espectáculo. Era el teatro del proceso, sin forma preconcebida. En el *Teatro del oprimido*, más que un guion cerrado, había una especie de infraestructura flexible que permitía improvisaciones, adiciones y omisiones. Entonces, siempre estaba sin terminar y la gente podía seguir agregando o quitando cosas. Finalmente, el valor de *Teatro del oprimido* residía en el proceso, no en el producto.

COAGULACIONES

> Estoy interesado en abordar el Tiempo en su existencia desestructurada. Es decir, estoy interesado en cómo esta bestia salvaje vive en la jungla, no en el zoológico. Estoy interesado en cómo el Tiempo existe antes de que pongamos nuestras patas sobre él —nuestras mentes, nuestra imaginación en él—.[32]

Los artefactos construidos a través de Talleres de Diseño y Construcción no pueden entenderse desde la forma *albertiana* de la disciplina, es decir, como un proceso que va desde la imagen preconcebida de una forma hacia su construcción. Estos artefactos son más bien momentos coagulados —de fuerzas, energías y materias— que emergen como resultado de un entramado múltiple y dialógico de voluntades humanas y no humanas a lo largo del tiempo. Esto supone un cambio de paradigma en la concepción del mundo material. En *On the nature of the universe*,[33] el poeta y filósofo romano Lucrecio concebía el mundo como una continuidad de materia-energía en la que todo —humanos y no humanos— estaba compuesto de una misma sustancia infinita y en la que se disponían todas las posibilidades.

> Revelaré aquellos *átomos* a partir de los cuales la naturaleza crea todas las cosas (…) A estos en mi discurso comúnmente les

doy nombres tales como materia prima, o cuerpos generativos o *semillas de las cosas*. O puedo llamarlas *partículas primarias*, porque aparecen primero y luego, todo lo demás está compuesto por ellas.[34]

En este mundo continuo, las materias-energías tendrían habilidades creativas que se expresarían en la capacidad inmanente de autoorganizarse y adquirir diferentes formas. Pero, ¿cómo estas materias-energías se autoorganizan hasta adquirir una forma de cosa? Jane Bennett[35] sugiere que existe un proceso de materialización en constante formación y reforma en virtud de una *vitalidad* intrínseca. En otras palabras, las materias-energías tienen su propia vitalidad que les permite autoorganizarse en cosas que también tienen su propia agencia y movimiento previsto con direccionalidad y causalidad.[36] Manuel Delanda,[37] por su parte, afirma que es un flujo que permite a la materia-energía autoorganizarse y adquirir forma contingente. Flujos dinámicos de materia-energía e información con cualidades semiestables y diferentes expresiones —geológicas, biológicas y lingüísticas— atraviesan cuerpos y poblaciones humanas y no humanas y se mineralizan dando forma a cosas del mundo material. Gilles Deleuze y Félix Guattari desarrollan el concepto de *agencements*[38] para explorar la capacidad de la materia-energía para formar estructuras a escalas macro.

Un *agencement* es una multiplicidad de interagencias de componentes heterogéneos —materiales y expresiones tangibles e intangibles— que interactúan y fluyen dando forma a *ensamblajes*, *estratos* o *cuerpos sin órganos*.[39] Pero, ¿qué hace que estos componentes permanezcan adheridos al *agencement*? Bennett rastrea esta pregunta en Spinoza, Serres y Deleuze y Guattari. Según ella, Spinoza vio una tendencia de la materia a moverse y dar origen a formas o cosas cuando se ve afectada por la agencia de otra cosa.[40] Según la autora, Michael Serres explica esa tendencia como la capacidad de la materia de «colisionar, congelar, transformarse, evolucionar y desintegrarse por la acción de la física».[41] Finalmente, Bennett destaca el concepto de Deleuze y Guattari de «nomadismo de la materia, o materia-movimiento, o materia en variación»[42] que entra y sale de los *agencement* por su nomadismo, así como por sus múltiples interacciones con otras entidades y fuerzas con diferente tasa de velocidad y ritmo de cambio.[43]

AGENCIAS ENTRELAZADAS

> Naturalmente, nadie se molestaría con estos estudios, si un ser llamado Odradek en realidad no existiera.[44]

La complejidad del entramado de fuerzas que engloban los *Talleres de Diseño y Construcción*, así como las manifestaciones materiales de los artefactos después de su materialización requieren de un análisis interagencial que las formas de producción de la arquitectura no tenían previsto. En su *Teoría del Actor en Red*, ANT, Bruno Latour[45] ofrece un enfoque semiótico de las interacciones sociales donde lo social se presenta como un tipo de conexión entre *actantes* humanos y no-humanos (actores sin figuración) en un marco de *agencias* distributivas. En este sentido, los no-humanos podrían desempeñar un papel tan activo en el mundo socio-material como el de los seres humanos. El autor propone una nueva rama de la sociología denominada *sociología de las asociaciones*, frente al tradicional campo estable y fijo de la sociología de lo social que ha olvidado o ignorado la existencia de entidades no humanas, y ha impuesto prefiguraciones a los agregados sociales e *interagencias*. Jane Bennett[46] afirma que los artículos hechos por el hombre o «no del todo cosas» tienen su propia agencia o una fuerza especial de independencia.[47] Son actantes con papel activo en la sociedad ya que tienen la capacidad de relacionar o incluso alterar cuerpos humanos y no humanos. Bennett describe la agencia de las cosas como *cosa-poder* y proporciona ejemplos específicos para demostrar que los materiales no humanos como actantes tienen un papel activo en la sociedad. La autora analiza las capacidades metamórficas de los escombros, la capacidad de la materia inorgánica para formar entidades y ensamblajes, la agencia de los actantes jurídicos —muestras, pruebas materiales y deodanos— como «algo que actúa o a quien otros le otorgan una actividad», o como «operador cuasi-causal».[48] Bennett también está interesada en comprender la agencia distribuida y el poder exponencial de los ensamblajes cuando las partes heterogéneas se unen e interactúan.[49] Ella apela al concepto de Spinoza de «cuerpos conativos» en los que los cuerpos aumentan su poder asociándose con otros[50] en un entramado mosaico complejo. De Deleuze y Guattari, Bennett toma prestado el término «cuerpos afectivos» en el sentido de que hay una vitalidad de la multiplicidad que aumenta cuando las entidades entran en colaboración, cooperación o interactividad con otros cuerpos y fuerzas. Para ilustrar cómo funciona la agencia dentro de los ensamblajes, Bennett trae el ejemplo de una red eléctrica en un apagón. En ese evento, unos generadores que inicialmente no estaban conectados al ensamblaje provocaron un cambio en los patrones de flujo de electrones que terminó en una inesperada concatenación de episodios más allá de la voluntad, las expectativas y el imaginario de los humanos

y, al mismo tiempo, obligaron a otros ac[...] a conectarse al ensamblaje.[51] Bennett llam[...] el *shi* de un ensamblaje vibratorio.

ANCLAJES

La forma visible de los animales no es[...] efecto, más que un disfraz. Cuando re[...] a sus hogares, lo hacen para despojars[...] su apariencia, cubriéndose con adorno[...] plumas y adornos ceremoniales [...].[52]

Las arquitecturas e infraestructur[...] construidas a partir de los Talleres de [...] y Construcción no intentan imponer una f[...] la materia para obtener un objeto. Más bie[...] tentan combinar materiales y redirigir s[...] de materia-energía en anticipación de lo q[...] dría surgir durante las correlaciones de [...] que involucran el proceso de coconstru[...] Siguiendo este pensamiento, debemos pens[...] obras como eventos que se solidifican a [...] de la experiencia del encuentro entre los [...] pos y el mundo material-natural. Tim Ingo[...] ría que «el proceso de génesis y crecimie[...] da origen a las formas en el mundo que hab[...] es más importante que la forma».[53] En *Mate[...] contra la materialidad*, Ingold[54] afirma [...] mundo es una especie de mar de materia-e[...] que está en constante flujo y correlac[...] fuerzas. Según Inglold, los seres human[...] humanos están destinados a sumergirse y [...] rimentar ese océano material mediante la [...] riencia práctica.[55] En *La textilidad del h[...] Ingold profundiza en la idea de la exper[...] práctica y afirma que el proceso de hacer [...] actuación en la que seguimos los flujos [...] materia con nuestros cuerpos por medio [...] vimientos que son «itinerantes, improv[...] y rítmicos»[57] Más adelante, en *Estar vivo[...] gold plantea que ese mar de materia-ener[...] coagula en hilos cuando son interceptad[...] entidades vivientes. Esos hilos son las h[...] de la vida a lo largo de los cuales tien[...] gar los procesos de vivir, crecer o hacer [...] una araña y su red. Una vez solidificadas [...] huellas no se pueden separar de su entor[...] las corrientes, fuerzas y presiones q[...] rodean. Como un barrilete en el aire. «E[...] dos de estas corrientes —es decir, red[...] a objetos— estarían muertos».[59] La histo[...] demostrado que un diseño podría ser espe[...] del sitio y, sin embargo, sus materias-en[...] podrían haber viajado de artefactos ante[...] y separarse de ellos en cualquier momen[...] trasladarse también a otro lugar en el f[...] Enric Miralles decía que las arquitectura[...] cosas no siempre están en su sitio y que [...] tros recuerdos viajan de un lugar a otro[...]

mismo modo, Henry Focillon argumentaría que las formas tienen vida propia y viajan de una entidad a otra, incluso cuando tienen diferentes orígenes genéticos.[61] Es decir, existe un medio, pero este no determina totalmente la identidad de las entidades porque, en parte, siempre existe nuestra subjetividad. Pero, además, las entidades tienen una identidad, un código interior que condiciona el medio y la forma en que se relacionan con él. Como decían Deleuze y Guattari, existen procesos de desterritorialización y descodificación en los que las entidades pierden parte de su código interno para poder trasladarse —reterritorializarse— de un entorno a otro.[62]

De acuerdo con Deleuze y Guattari, el grado de codificación y territorialización depende de los diferenciales de intensidades y correlación de fuerzas entre líneas de segmentación y líneas de fuga que desvían lo que ellos llaman *Plan de consistencia*. Podríamos decir que el *Plan de consistencia* tiene el mismo espíritu metafísico que la primera etapa del mundo de Lucrecio e Ingold. Deleuze y Guattari dicen que su *Plan de consistencia* es omnipresente y trazado por una *máquina abstracta* que opera en un estado original caracterizado por un continuo virtual de materia-energía que contenía en un principio todas las posibilidades.[63] Sin embargo, este *Plan de consistencia* podría ser transformado por las *máquinas de guerra* que catalizan los flujos para crear las condiciones para la transformación.[64] Es decir, los movimientos de materia-energía son procesos de territorialización/desterritorialización, codificación/descodificación que son desplegados por las *máquinas de guerra* por medio de líneas de segmentación y de fuga.[65] Deleuze y Guattari relacionan las *máquinas de guerra* con los movimientos insurgentes y nómadas, quienes, al habitar y transitar por el territorio, propician la interrupción y reverberación de cambios de aquellas condiciones omnipresentes iniciales.

DISCUSIONES

Sordidez, de la serie Los Monstruos Cósmicos, 1964. Construcción en polymatter a base de madera —armazón general y piezas lisas y puntiagudas—, metales —acero, hierro, frenos de bicicleta, proyectores de flash antiguos, remates de cabecera y tapones de soda—, cartón, plástico, raíces secas de arbustos, uñas y esmalte. Plataforma incluida, 129 x 120 x 400 cm.[66]

Las condiciones presentes en el *Sur global* y, en Argentina en particular, desestabilizan las correlaciones fijas y directas enunciadas por Deleuze y Guattari respecto a la burocracia gubernamental y a las fuerzas jerárquicas, las representaciones de paredes blancas y agujeros negros, líneas de fuga y líneas de segmentación. Podríamos decir que, dado que las fuerzas jerárquicas del poder real son altamente fluidas, invisibles y operan para desestabilizar, desterritorializar y decodificar, la insurgencia debe actuar en sentido contrario. En la actualidad, el poder real está desligado de los Estados, instituciones, gobiernos, partidos políticos y territorios, y se mueve con fluidez para drenar el mundo. Después de succionar al mundo lo suficiente, se desvanecen en el aire o se esconden en paraísos fiscales. Durante los gobiernos progresistas, las instituciones suelen ser conformadas y estabilizadas por movimientos autoorganizados y las fuerzas jerárquicas funcionan inyectando flujos para desterritorializar y decodificar. En este sentido, capitalismo e insurgencia podrían operar alternativamente con las formas y acciones del otro y utilizar todo el abanico de posibilidades que alguna vez existió para operar en las correlaciones de fuerzas. Las relaciones entre medios y fines, estrategias y tácticas, ideologías y políticas, son hoy en día altamente complejas y contradictorias. La alienación hegemónica y los montajes opresores no pueden ser expuestos, fracturados y desmontados de golpe como pensábamos durante los años sesenta y setenta. Por eso, la proliferación de líneas de fuga que sugieren Deleuze y Guattari como vehículos para la emancipación, ahora nos pueden llevar a la muerte. La tarea es aprender a ser y moverse en el mundo de forma inesperada y abordar una combinación de múltiples escalas y velocidades espacio-temporales para subvertir y desestabilizar las estructuras hegemónicas que subyugan a la humanidad.

En términos *deleuzianos*, hemos descubierto cómo hacer proliferar agujeros negros en paredes blancas y cómo multiplicar paredes blancas en agujeros negros. Necesitamos encontrar el modo de movilizar más líneas de segmentaciones para organizarnos, hasta ver la oportunidad de penetrar el sistema por las puertas de atrás a través de líneas de fuga. Eso es lo que llamo la *estrategia del río revuelto* o la *resistencia in medias res*. Por eso, Deleuze y Guattari afirman que la transformación no debe ser un gesto demasiado violento

ya que destruir los estratos sin prudencia nos arrastrará a la catástrofe. Lo peor entonces no sería quedarnos estratificados —organizados, significados, sujetos— sino precipitar los estratos en un derrumbe suicida o insano, que los haga caer sobre nosotros, como una carga definitiva.[67] Solo así, manteniendo una relación minuciosa con los estratos, es posible liberar las líneas de fuga, hacer pasar y dejar huir los flujos conjugados […].[68]

La tarea primordial de los *Talleres de Diseño y Construcción* llevados a cabo por el colectivo Matéricos Periféricos ha sido contribuir a que germinen posibilidades críticas para romper poco a poco la continuidad y totalidad de los falsos montajes hegemónicos que impiden el desarrollo de un mundo más justo y equitativo. En esta dirección, pensamos que las fuentes de cualquier posibilidad de novedad en el sentido de la creatividad y la emancipación de esos falsos montajes se encuentran solo en las periferias, las grietas del sistema, sus fragmentos y restos, las ruinas, la basura, los cuerpos racializados, feminizados y las historias de perdedores y oprimidos. En ese sentido, los *Talleres de Diseño y Construcción* pueden ser entendidos como prácticas colectivas de diseño decolonial ya que pueden ayudar a hacer posible localizar, desenterrar, identificar y visualizar esos fragmentos y restos, discernir formas de ensamblarlos, imaginar mundos alternativos a partir de ellos y, eventualmente, coagularlos en artefactos. Estos artefactos son concebidos como orquestaciones y convivencias de contenidos y expresiones emergentes —materia-energía, fuerzas, ideas, velocidades, informaciones y variables de todo tipo— que fluyen y son interceptadas por nuestros cuerpos al realizar acciones *in situ* e *in vivo* que las ordenan y coagulan en multiplicidades contingentes e inestables.

Nuestros *Talleres de Diseño y Construcción* se ocupan, usualmente, de la coconstrucción de artefactos para sustentar las instituciones locales en sus actividades comunitarias, desafiar a la agencia estatal, devolver tierras públicas a la comunidad y activar pequeñas cooperativas y empresas. Son equipamientos comunitarios, como comedores, capillas, centros comunitarios, infraestructuras deportivas. Además, son instrumentos para contribuir a la construcción de comunidad, a la organización popular, a los procesos colectivos de autoconciencia y emancipación. Los artefactos son una manifestación física de nuestra interacción con esos procesos, así como las coexistencias, negociaciones y destilaciones de las ideas, necesidades, sueños y habilidades de todos los y las participantes. No tienen presencia absoluta porque son tanto manifestaciones históricas como expresiones de futuros posibles.

El aspecto mestizo, inacabado y complejo de los artefactos atiende a traducciones materiales de fenómenos tangibles e intangibles, y también a un cuerpo de procedimientos capaces de generar una coconstrucción dialógica colectiva. Es como si los artefactos hubieran catalizado esos procesos y contingencias. Es decir, se abren a esos futuros y devenires posibles. Aparecen disruptivos, incómodos, indisciplinados, con proliferaciones y acumulaciones abridoras. Están hechos con los materiales que están a la mano: polvo, metales, ladrillos donados, reciclados, descartados o incluso partes desechadas compuestas de otros artefactos. Sus formas no se corresponden con los parámetros de la estética de lo terminado o acabado, ni de la búsqueda de una totalidad. No necesitan un relato único, o una gran idea, ni una racionalidad que vincule estructura-espacio-fachada exterior de forma lineal. No hay prefiguración en el proceso de materialización. No hay una definición *a priori* de la forma. Más bien, existe un método dialógico *in situ*, *in vivo* que permite la coexistencia de lo opuesto y lo diverso, dando lugar a nuevos mundos colectivos posibles. Un mundo donde existan todos los mundos. Es por ello que los artefactos coconstruidos podrían ser definidos como ensamblajes en movimiento o transformación y cuya configuración en cualquier momento es el resultado de seguir contingencias —mutaciones—, variables, accidentes y negociaciones. Los artefactos son un proceso de presente infinito en el que la correlación de fuerzas se manifiesta por medio de la orquestación de dinámicas, el manejo de la contingencia, la expresión de lo disponible y la amplificación de lo colectivo. El valor de los artefactos coconstruidos reside en el proceso, no en el producto.

Finalmente, nuestros artefactos tienen la capacidad de mutar o ser informados por nuevos materiales e ideas. Siempre se encuentran un poco desgarrados, inacabados y abiertos, de modo que permiten nuevos procesos de mediación entre elementos heterogéneos, así como ulteriores interpretaciones, mutilaciones, añadidos, incluso conservando cierto grado de identidad y consistencia. Además, muchos artefactos siguen creciendo en el espacio y la materia, otros son cortados o modificados, muchos son destruidos, quemados o desmontados. Algunas de sus partes son traducidas o transportadas a otros lugares y transformadas o ensambladas en otras cosas. Pocos de ellos simplemente se rompen, son absorbidos por la naturaleza, se descomponen o se convierten en nuevas materias primas. También expanden las reverberaciones más allá de su entorno físico inmediato. Algunos artefactos provocan mejoras de infraestructura adicionales en el vecindario. Su presencia física obliga a intervenciones públicas o a nuevos trabajos comunitarios que de otro modo serían inimaginables. Una vez coagulados, los artefactos muestran comportamientos que podrían asimilarse a una agencia interna o vitalidad. En la mayoría de los casos, estos artefactos funcionan como punto de partida para posteriores procesos de cambio social y material en el territorio sin la intervención directa de los seres humanos. Es decir, tienen su propia agencia.

1. Mi traducción de Bell Hooks. *Theory as liberatory practice* (Yale: Yale JL & Feminism 4, 1991).

2. Ver Matéricos Periféricos www.matericosweb.com

3. Bell Hooks, *Theory as liberatory practice*. (Yale JL & Feminism 4, 1991).

4. Paulo Freire, *Pedagogía de la indignación: cartas pedagógicas en un mundo revuelto*. (Buenos Aires: Siglo veintiuno editores, 2012) 47.

5. David Harvey, *The 'new' imperialism: accumulation by dispossession* (Oxford: Oxford University, 2003).

6. Chu, Cecilia L. y Romola Sanyal. *Spectacular cities of our time*. Geoforum No. 65, 2015, 399-402.

7. Julio Cortázar y Juan Fresán, *Casa tomada* (Buenos Aires: Ediciones Minotauro, 1969).

8. Julio Cortázar, *La Prosa del Observatorio* (Buenos Aires: Archipiélago Books, 1972).

9. Manuel DeLanda, *A thousand years of nonlinear history*. Jonathan Crary, Stanford Kwinter, and Bruce Mau, editors. (New York: Swerve Editions, 2000).

10. Gilles Deleuze y Felix Guattari, *Mil mesetas. Capitalismo y esquizofrenia*, trad. José Velázquez Pérez. (Valencia: Pre-textos, 2002).

11. Ernesto Cardenal. *Los ovnis de oro: Poemas indios*, México: Siglo XXI, 1998, 48.

12. Mi traducción de Cecilia L. Chu y Romola Sanyal. "Spectacular cities of our time", *Geoforum* No. 65. 2015, 399-402.

13. Richard Falk, "Resisting globalization from above through globalization from below. Globalization and the Politics of Resistance". *International Political Economy Series*, ed. Gills B.K. (London: Palgrave Macmillan, 2000).

14. Manfred Max-Neef. U.S. Is becoming an under developing nation, filmado en septiembre de 2010, https://www.youtube.com/watch?v=hjcbBnM2OUo

15. Seo Bongman, "Borrowing Money. Aid, debt and dependence", en *A world of Difference. Encountering and contesting development*, ed. Enric Shepperd, Philip W. Porter, David R. Faust and Richa Nagar. (New York: the Ghilford Press, 2009), 559-593.

16. Faranak Miraftab, "Insurgent Practices and Decolonization of Future(s)" en *The Routledge Handbook of Planning Theory*, ed. Michael Gunder, Ali Madanipour and Vanessa Watson. (London: Routledge, 2017) 276-288.

17. Saul Yurkiévich, *La movediza modernidad* (Madrid: Santillana S.A, 1996), 336. En este extracto se refiere al trabajo de Ernesto Cardenal.

18. Mi traducción de Jennings, Deherty and Levin, ed., op. cit., 25.

19. Jennings, Deherty, and Levin, ed., op. cit.

20. Adorno, Theodor W., *Teoría estética*, trad. Jorge Navarro Pérez. Madrid: Ediciones Akal, 2004

21. Jennings, Deherty, and Levin, ed., op. cit., 24.

22. Mi traducción de Jennings, Deherty, and Levin, ed., op. cit., 39.

23. Deleuze y Guattari, op. cit.

24. En aquello que las personas esquizofrénicas no separan su cuerpo del mundo y escapan de la interpretación simplista triangular freudiana de las relaciones hijo-mami-papi, así como del mecanismo de contención del deseo. Para Deleuze y Guattari todos somos máquinas de deseo.

25. En *Mille Plateaux* (el libro original en francés) Deleuze y Guattari hablan de *agencement* como las agencias o conexiones y relaciones entre componentes, más que como la forma específica en que los componentes se ensamblan físicamente. Es de este *agencement* que pueden surgir estratos, ensamblajes o *cuerpos sin órganos*.

26. Manuel DeLanda, *New philosophy of society. Assemblage theory and social complexity*. (New York: Bloomsbury Publishing, 2019) 19. También ver: *A Comparison of Deleuze's Assemblage Theory and the New Materialist Approach* at Assemblage Thinking Symposium 2017, University of the Aegean - Depart. of Geography (GR) recorded and available at https://www.youtube.com/watch?v=VzJqOX4ASA8

27. Godofredo Iommi M., *Carta del errante*. (Valparaíso: Escuela de Arquitectura UCV, 1976) 9.

28. Michael W. Jennings et al. Walter Benjamin, ed. *The work of art in the age of its technological reproducibility and other writings on media*, trad. Edmund Jephcott, Rodney Livingstone, Howard Eiland, and others. (Cambridge: The Belknap Press of Harvard University Press, 2008) 30.

29. Cecilia Boal, profesora y directora de teatro que fue pareja de Augusto Boal durante 40 años dice que el título original del libro como escribió Augusto Boal era *Poéticas políticas*. Escuchar su conferencia en el Critical 13/13. Critical theory texts. 13 seminars at Columbia. http://blogs.law.columbia.edu/critique1313/4-13/

30. Augusto Boal, *Teatro del oprimido* (México: Talleres Gráficos Continental S.A., 1989).

31. Augusto Boal, op. cit., 12

32. Mi traducción de B.H. Friedman, ed., *Give My Regards to Eighth Street. Collected Writings of Morton Feldman*. (Cambridge: Extract Change, 2000) 87.

33. Lucretius. *On the nature of universe*, trad. Roland Latham. (Melbourne, London, Baltimor: Pinguin Book, 1951).

34. Mi traducción de Lucretius, op. cit., 28.

35. Bennett, Jane. *Vibrant Matter: A Political Ecology of Things*. Durham: Duke University Press, 2010

36. Bennett, op. cit., xviii.

37. Manuel DeLanda, op. cit.

38. Deleuze y Guattari, op. cit.

39. Deleuze y Guattari afirman que la diferencia entre ensamblajes, estratos y cuerpo sin órganos está determinada por la intensidad de dos variables: territorialización-desterritorialización, y codificación -descodificación. Altas intensidades de territorialización y codificación tienden a conformar estratos, y bajas intensidades, *cuerpo sin órganos*. En un estado intermedio, ensamblajes.

40. Bennett, op. cit., x.

41. Mi traducción de Bennett, op. cit., xi.

42. Mi traducción de Bennett, op. cit., 54.

43. Bennett, op. cit., 18.

44. Franz Kafka, *Las preocupaciones de un padre de familia*. (BoD-Books on Demand, 2016).

45. Bruno Latour, *Reassembling the Social: An*

Introduction to Actor-Network-Theory. (New York: Oxford University Press, 2005).

46. Bennett, op. cit.

47. Bennett, op. cit. xvi.

48. Mi traducción de Bennett, op. cit., 9.

49. Es decir, el poder del todo es mayor que el de la suma de las partes.

50. Bennett, op. cit., 21.

51. Tales como movilizando equipos políticos y técnicos durante el corte para resolver la situación.

52. Philippe Descola. *Más allá de naturaleza y cultura,* trad. Horacio Pons. (Buenos Aires-Madrid: Amorrortu editores, 2012) 32

53. Ingold, op. cit., 91.

54. Tim Ingold, "Materials against materiality". *Archaeological Dialogues No. 14* (1) (2007): 1-16.

55. Ingold, op. cit.

56. Tim Ingold. "The textility of making". *Cambridge Journal of Economics No. 34* (2010): 91-102, 91.

57. Ingold, op. cit.

58. Tim Ingold. *Being alive: Essays on movement, knowledge and description* (New York: Routledge, 2011), 89-95.

59. Ingold, op. cit., 93.

60. EMBT Miralles Tagliabue, *Obras y proyectos* (Milán: Skira Editore, 2002).

61. Henri Focillo,.*The Life of Forms in Art* (New York: Wittenbor, Shultz, Inc., 1948).

62. Deleuze y Guattari, op. cit., 47-81.

63. Deleuze y Guattari, op. cit.

64. Deleuze y Guattari, op. cit., 359-433.

65. Deleuze y Guattari, op. cit.

66. Antonio Berni, Fundación Malba. Museo de Arte Latinoamericano de Buenos Aires. http://www.malba.org.ar/antinio-berni-juanito-y-ramona/

67. Deleuze y Guattari, op. cit., 165.

68. Deleuze y Guattari, op. cit., 166.

Aprendiendo de Latinoamérica

JOSÉ LUIS URIBE ORTIZ

1

En el año 2010, la exposición *Small Scale, Big Change: New Architectures of Social Engagement* presentó once proyectos[1] y obras ubicadas en los cinco continentes. La exposición fue curada por Andres Lepik y estuvo conformada por arquitecturas que promovían una nueva manera de habitar en el entorno construido de las comunidades periféricas y desatendidas. Los procesos de diseño y construcción exhibidos en la exposición fueron desarrollados mediante un trabajo colaborativo entre los arquitectos y los habitantes, quienes se reconocen como articuladores de un proceso de transformación social, económico y político, configurados a partir de obras de pequeña escala. Parte de la nota de prensa de la exposición declara,

Además de los nuevos modos de diseño participativo, los proyectos en exhibición incorporan prácticas ecológicas y socialmente sostenibles pioneras específicas del sitio, inclu[ye] la exploración de materiales nuevos y tradicionales. Las poblaciones que anteriormente rara vez habían recibido la atención de los arquitectos se dedica[n] diseños que incorporan innovación dig[na] de la atención más amplia. El renovado compromiso de estos arquitectos y de muchos de sus colegas con la arquitec[tura] socialmente responsable recuerda los ideales de los maestros del siglo XX, pero estos diseñadores evitan los mode[los] utópicos y generales de sus predeceso[res] para el cambio impuesto desde arriba. *Small Scale, Big Change* presenta proy[ectos] acupunturales radicalmente pragmátic[os], intervenciones limitadas con efectos [de] amplio alcance.[2]

Revisando parte de la curaduría de [...] se reconoce a un grupo de arquitectos qu[e tienen] tienen como actitud común la formulación [de una] arquitectura basada en lo artesanal como [lógica] operativa en un entorno caracterizado por l[a vul]nerabilidad y escasez. La imagen del arqu[itecto] se sitúa como un articulador de cambio s[ocial] mediante un proceso colaborativo basad[o en la] construcción artesanal, promoviendo una [arqui]tectura de baja tecnología y que recono[ce como] referente técnico las antiguas prácticas [cons]tructivas. Cuatro años después, y bajo un e[nfoque] similar, se exhibe en el Museo ICO de Madr[id, The] *Architect is present*, curada por Luis F[ernán]dez-Galiano. La exhibición reúne cinco es[tudios] internacionales[3], cuyas obras persiguen [el ob]jetivo de cubrir las necesidades de la so[ciedad] aprovechando al máximo los recursos dispon[ibles]. El interés de la exposición se centra en e[l modo] que toman materiales humildes y nobles c[omo el] barro, el bambú, la madera y la cerámica, y [como] parte de una arquitectura que promueve un [encuentro] basado en las técnicas constructivas lo[cales]. Revisamos el testimonio de Luis Fernández-[Galia]no, en su condición de curador de la exhib[ición].

La exposición muestra la obra de cinco [...] influyentes estudios internacionales [que] han hecho de la austeridad su referent[e] ético y estético. Extendidos por los c[inco] continentes, estos jóvenes arquitect[os] trabajan en entornos de economía prec[aria] mostrando que la escasez de recursos p[uede] ser un estímulo para la inventiva técn[ica] y la participación comunitaria, y el [...] fundamento de una arquitectura respon[sable] donde la vocación de servicio no excluya la belleza y la emoción.[4]

Ambas exposiciones son el retrato de los temas de interés común en un grupo particular de arquitectos contemporáneos, lo que abre la discusión hacia el sentido social de la arquitectura y el retorno de los valores artesanales en la construcción que emerge de los entornos vulnerables.

2

De lo anterior se desprende la idea de que durante los últimos veinte años, la contingencia política y las crisis económicas han orientado la escena arquitectónica contemporánea hacia contextos periféricos, promoviendo una arquitectura surgida bajo ámbitos de escasez y articulada por sus abundantes recursos materiales. Esta condición ha sido revisada en diferentes publicaciones de arquitectura, exposiciones y congresos provenientes del primer mundo, que se han centrado en una condición latinoamericana de una arquitectura poscrisis. Es así como podemos mencionar revistas como AV Monografías N° 138, Latin America 2010- España 2009; A+U N° 532, Latin America; 25 Projects, (Japón, 2015); o Harvard Design Magazine N° 34, (EE. UU., 2011).

Se suman iniciativas curatoriales como las versiones del Freshlatino, (España, 2009 y 2015), comisariada por Ariadna Cantis; las distintas versiones de la Bienal Latinoamericana de Arquitectura, España; el simposio Latitudes, Architecture in the Americas, EE. UU.; o el Mies Crown Hall Americas Prize, EE. UU. En cada uno de estos formatos de difusión y reflexión en torno a la arquitectura latinoamericana se reconoce como elemento común la práctica arquitectónica de oficinas y colectivos de arquitectura que hasta años atrás se promovían bajo un rótulo de emergentes, como A77, Argentina; Plan: b arquitectos, Colombia; Al Borde, Ecuador; Lab.Pro. Fab, Venezuela; Lukas Fuster, Paraguay; entre otros. En ese sentido, la portada la revista C3 N° 295, (Corea, 2009), retrata de una manera elocuente el proceso de cambio territorial que experimenta Latinoamérica, al editar un monográfico en torno a Medellín y Talca. Estos contextos contrapuestos dan cuenta, por un lado, de una generación de jóvenes arquitectos emergentes colombianos y, por otro lado, de la formulación de un innovador modelo académico basado en la práctica. En ambos casos se reconoce la construcción de un territorio y una atención por el proyecto arquitectónico asociado a la dimensión pública.

De forma progresiva, Latinoamérica define una nueva narrativa arquitectónica, orientada por la incidencia de lo artesanal como parte activa de la obra que promueve el habitar público. Ha surgido una arquitectura al margen, articulada mediante pequeñas iniciativas dirigidas por diversos laboratorios de enseñanza de arquitectura que han trabajado con las comunidades, lo que ha sumado a la discusión el aporte de Latinoamérica a la condición contemporánea de la arquitectura.

3

Durante la XI Bienal Iberoamericana de Arquitectura y Urbanismo tuve la oportunidad de entrevistar a dieciocho arquitectos, editores y críticos de arquitectura vinculados a la escena contemporánea latinoamericana. En la habitación de un hotel ubicado en el centro histórico de Asunción, Paraguay, cada uno de ellos contestaba a una pregunta en común: ¿Qué aporta Latinoamérica a la condición contemporánea de la arquitectura?[5]

Carlos Quintans, antiguo editor de la revista Obradoiro, citaba al fallecido Paulo Mendes da Rocha, quien planteaba que en Latinoamérica estaba la posibilidad de inventar el mundo. Considerando esa sentencia como margen de acción, algunas escuelas de arquitectura latinoamericanas han asumido un papel fundamental al reformular el paisaje arquitectónico desde una arquitectura de pequeña escala, diseñada y construida por los estudiantes, en colaboración con pequeñas comunidades, formando nuevos arquitectos atentos a la búsqueda de oportunidades de proyectos que se adecuan a la escasez de recursos. Se ha replanteado el papel del arquitecto en la sociedad y en esa línea aparecen diversas prácticas académicas que han surgido en el continente durante los últimos diez años, entre los que se destacan Matéricos Periféricos (Argentina, 2001); la Obra de Titulación de la Escuela de Arquitectura de la Universidad de Talca (Chile, 2004); el Taller de Al Borde, en la Universidad Tecnológica Indoamericana (Ecuador, 2016); el Taller Activo, del Tecnológico de Monterrey/Querétaro (México, 2010); y el Taller Nubes de Madera de la Facultad de Arquitectura de la Universidad Pontificia Bolivariana, (Colombia, 2013), por citar algunos.

4

Por otro lado, gran parte de los arquitectos y despachos de arquitectura que surgieron en Latinoamérica a mediados de la última década, han encontrado en la academia un espacio de refugio y exploración en torno a la realidad poscrisis económica. Ha quedado a un lado la arquitectura del edificio público y la segunda vivienda, dando espacio para que las instancias de experimentación proyectual y constructiva se desarrollen en entornos comunitarios asociados a la periferia. Es así como las obras construidas desde las prácticas académicas a lo largo de la región se sitúan en contextos incómodos, en aquella realidad que Glauber Rocha describió exquisitamente en su manifiesto *Estética del hambre* (1965)

> De *Aruanda a Vidas secas*, el *cinema novo* narró, describió, poetizó, discursó, analizó, excitó, los temas del hambre: personajes comiendo tierra, personajes comiendo raíces, personajes robando para comer, personajes matando para comer, personajes huyendo para comer, personajes sucios, feos, descarnados, viviendo en casas sucias, feas, oscuras. Fue esta galería de hambrientos que identificó el *cinema novo* con el miserabilísimo tan condenado por el gobierno, por la crítica al servicio de los intereses antinacionales, por los productores y por el público […] [6]

Son contextos próximos para los estudiantes, quienes desde el conocimiento de esa realidad logran desarrollar una arquitectura de la resistencia, de bajo costo, de pequeña escala y gran impacto social. Es ahí donde radica su complejidad.

5

Los estudiantes latinoamericanos tienen la experiencia de habitar los lugares sobre los que proyectan y construyen, lo que les da la autoridad para experimentar. No se trata de construir solo por la fascinación en el obrar, sino que formulan proyectos que abordan diversas dimensiones, como la exploración técnica o la aproximación a entornos sociales vulnerables. Estas condiciones permiten articular la figura del futuro arquitecto latinoamericano como un mediador entre el habitante y su entorno cultural. Un arquitecto que participa como un intermediario que trata de vincularse en todas las etapas del proyecto, desde la interacción directa con el habitante o colaborando en el montaje constructivo, promoviendo un ánimo colectivo propio de la fase de construcción de una obra. Esta actitud, propia de una arquitectura de la cooperación, la podemos reconocer en diversos contextos periféricos de Latinoamérica donde, de manera aislada, algunas escuelas de arquitectura han desarrollado una práctica académica basada en la reciprocidad.

Bajo esta lógica, es destacable que este proceso colaborativo entre los estudiantes y el contexto comunitario se configure por medio de los materiales que caracterizan un entorno puntual, ya que cada objeto arquitectónico aglutina la materia de ese contexto, sin ornamentos, de manera cruda y sincera, manifestando la honestidad de la tierra, el ladrillo y la madera.

Sin embargo, esta lógica constructiva no de lado la exploración de materiales contemp neos asociados a la artificialidad propi producción industrial. La exploración ma plantea nuevas posibilidades tecnológica arquitectura, pero condicionada por la ec de recursos de los que se dispone. Al no optar por la alta tecnología, aparece el r humano más económico que es el oficio incr en las manos de los estudiantes tras su co te adiestramiento, en colaboración con l rramientas proyectuales, digitales y fí Respecto a esto último Juhani Pallasmaa p

> La herramienta es una extensión y una especialización de la mano que altera posibilidades y capacidades naturale Cuando se utiliza un hacha o un cuchil el usuario diestro no piensa en la man la herramienta como entidades diferen separadas; la herramienta se ha desarrollado para ser parte de la man ha transformado en una especie de órga totalmente nuevo, una mano herramient

Hay que mencionar que todas las obra venientes de los talleres prácticos la mericanos corresponden a operas primas, que es destacable la manera en que el de asociado a la manipulación de recursos re dos o de desecho, adquiere valor como exp arquitectónica. El chorreo del mortero o el parche, son rasgos de una arquite construida con la mano, que aportan rugos vibración a las superficies de los muros, y suelos. Estas manifestaciones propias puesta en obra, aportan un valor a la dim háptica dentro de los recorridos espacia cada una de las obras que forman parte d arquitectura. Las superficies de las ob exhiben con la sinceridad propia de u quitectura sin piel. Esto permite aprec arquitectura proveniente de los labora académicos latinoamericanos como prim considerando la referencia de Adrian para quien el concepto primitivo no es u mino políticamente correcto y tiende a de aquello que describe. [8] Son obras que ba belleza en lo primitivo, una belleza en l grado, propia de una arquitectura al marge acotado presupuesto y materiales recic aportando a la arquitectura contemporá valor de lo local. Es así como estas prá arquitectónicas abrazadas por la academi que conformar una escena de arquitectura que se encuentran en una trinchera. Una tr ra que cultiva una arquitectura de resist que busca imponerse a los modelos arquite cos establecidos por la globalización.

6

Volviendo a la perdida habitación de aquel céntrico hotel de Asunción, Paraguay, Carlos Pita, refiriéndose a Latinoamérica declamaba

> Aquí encontré que había de dónde agarrarse. Que había una emoción en el cuidado del material y hasta en el entendimiento de una cierta presencia de los objetos y una cierta monumentalidad. Una vez leí una entrevista a Sam Peckinpah cuando proyecta la película *Grupo salvaje —The wild bunch*, 1969—. Una señora lo acusa diciendo que hay mucha violencia y que es muy explícita. —El director le dice: Disculpe señora, pero es que cuando te disparan… sangras. Yo creo que la arquitectura latinoamericana es una arquitectura que sangra. Es una arquitectura que afronta la realidad y, sobre todo, transforma la realidad. El aporte de Latinoamérica a la condición contemporánea de la arquitectura es el hecho de ser capaz de producir una arquitectura con fuerte enraizamiento en lo local. Frente a una globalización y el *marketing*, yo creo que la arquitectura latinoamericana tiene la capacidad de aportar lugar. Huele a tierra.[9]

Considerando las palabras de Pita, cabe destacar que el valor de las prácticas académicas latinoamericanas se basa en la experimentación constructiva, donde los estudiantes junto a la comunidad indagan en la innovación técnica, valiéndose de un proceso guiado por el ensayo y error. Este proceso da cuenta de los riesgos que asumen estos laboratorios de arquitectura en cada uno de sus procesos de obra, donde llevan al extremo cada sistema constructivo con la finalidad de explorar las posibilidades formales, estructurales y constructivas de un material en particular, sin repetir repertorios utilizados en obras anteriores.

1. Los despachos que formaron parte de esta exhibición corresponden a Diébédo Francis Kéré, Burkina Faso; Elemental, Chile; Noero Wolff Architects, Sudáfrica; Anna Heringer, Alemania; Michael Maltzan Architecture, Estados Unidos; Hashim Sarkis A.L.U.D., Líbano; Rural Studio, Estados Unidos; Urban Think Tank, Venezuela; Jorge Mario Jáuregui, Brasil; Frédéric Druot, Anne Lacaton, and Jean Philippe Vassal, Francia; Estudio Teddy Cruz, Estados Unidos.
2. Andres Lepik y Barry Bergdoll, *Small Scale, Big Change: New Architectures of Social Engagement*. (New York, EE. UU.: The Museum of Modern Art, 2010) 4.
3. Los despachos que formaron parte de esta exhibición corresponden a Diébédo Francis Kéré, Burkina Faso; TYIN Tegnestue Architects, Noruega; Anupama Kundoo, India; Solano Benítez, Paraguay;y Anna Heringer, Alemania.
4. Luis Fernández- Galiano, *The architect is present* (Madrid, España: Avisa / Museo ICO, 2014) 7.
5. Estas entrevistas forman parte de *Feos, sucios y malos: Una mirada hacia la arquitectura latinoamericana contemporánea*, corresponde a un ensayo crítico arquitectónico que tiene como formato el audiovisual. El proyecto indaga por el actual estado de la arquitectura latinoamericana a partir del testimonio de reconocidos arquitectos que se reunieron en Asunción, Paraguay, durante la XI Bienal Internacional de Arquitectura y Urbanismo desarrollada en octubre de 2019. Conceptualmente, el cuerpo del relato audiovisual apuesta por la reducción: una cantidad limitada de destacados arquitectos que coinciden en una ciudad. Una habitación de hotel como locación. De manera libre, cada arquitecto responde a solo una pregunta formulada. Se utiliza una puesta en cámara en plano general, nivel fijo, sin movimiento. El referente directo de este ejercicio audiovisual corresponde a *Room 666* (1982) de Wim Wenders.
6. http://medina502.com/classes/lafilm_2014/readings/Glauber_Rocha_Estetica_del_hambre.pdf
7. Juhani. Pallasmaa, *La mano que piensa* (Barcelona: Editorial Gustavo Gili, 2012).
8. Adrian Forty *Primitivo, La palabra y el concepto*. Santiago, Chile: Ediciones ARQ. 2018, p. 9
9. Extracto de la conversación entre Carlos Pita y José Luis Uribe, en Asunción, Paraguay, el 8 de octubre de 2019. Documento grabado y transcrito.

El camino del aprendizaje comunitario

GUSTAVO DIÉGUEZ

Durante los años recientes, en el contexto de la enseñanza de la arquitectura en Latinoamérica, se han ido multiplicando diversas iniciativas académicas que tienen como objetivo construir piezas arquitectónicas en verdadera magnitud. A la luz de los resultados alcanzados por ellas, algunos de los cuales están recopilados en este libro, la primera pregunta que surge es, ¿por qué estas experiencias no han sido más habituales en tantos años de historia?

Es probable que el énfasis en la autonomía del proyecto que alentaron las teorías arquitectónicas más influyentes de la última mitad del siglo veinte tengan algún nivel de incidencia en cómo una buena parte de las unidades académicas universitarias decidieron tomar cierta distancia de la dimensión material táctil de la arquitectura en sus procesos de aprendizaje de la actividad proyectual. Tal vez por ese motivo es que los medios de representación arquitectónica en sus diversas variantes mantienen aún el control total del concepto del proyecto, dejando a un lado la posibilidad del acceso a una experiencia multidimensional que incluso exceda a la propia disciplina. Para aquella tradición de la enseñanza del proyecto es suficiente con el uso exclusivo de las herramientas gráficas y de la modelización a escala para cumplir con sus objetivos.

¿Cuál sería entonces la potencia que contienen las prácticas constructivas realizadas en contextos académicos para el aprendizaje de la disciplina arquitectónica? Si ponemos atención a la estructura de los planes de estudio, un argumento a favor lo constituye el hecho de que la materialización en tiempo real de las ideas proyectadas resulta ser una forma efectiva de conseguir la necesaria verificación del aprendizaje de los contenidos académicos que aparecen disueltos en las diversas materias de estudio.

Resulta frecuente escuchar críticas en las escuelas latinoamericanas de arquitectura respecto a la disociación existente entre campos del saber arquitectónico, acerca de la separación de los contenidos tecnológicos respecto a los del campo proyectual. La cuestión referida a la falta de integración de los conocimientos curriculares de las áreas temáticas a lo largo de los años que comprende la carrera de arquitectura, suele ser uno de los lugares comunes en las evaluaciones de las planificaciones académicas.

El vínculo estrecho del diseño con la experiencia de la dimensión constructiva de la arquitectura permite que la noción de proyecto sea parte activa de todo el proceso. Y que a partir de ello podamos comprender las nociones de ajuste y optimización de recursos que conlleva esa tarea. Los ejemplos reunidos en esta antología de casos demuestran desde cada una de sus miradas diferentes maneras específicas de reconocer el hecho construido como materia de aprendizaje.

Dentro de ese panorama, este texto debe comprenderse como un núcleo de consideraciones devenidas de las experiencias particulares, acumuladas en este tipo de prácticas constructivas educativas realizadas desde nuestra actividad en el Estudio a77.

En el camino de construcción de la teoría de una práctica, la intención de este escrito es poner de manifiesto el carácter de oportunidad que esta línea de trabajo pedagógico ofrece para que la arquitectura desempeñe un papel mediador en el aprendizaje comunitario de los modos de habitar, posibilitando escenarios de reflexión para encontrar la mayor precisión en cada experiencia.

La realización de intervenciones en enclaves concretos invita a estudiantes y profesores a ver aquello que los rodea con detenimiento, y a entender la naturaleza del campo de acción que surge como consecuencia. De este modo, el aprendizaje de la arquitectura emerge como una actividad reflexiva sobre los modos de vida en común. Ese componente de índole pedagógica cobra mayor relevancia cuando dirigimos la mirada hacia contextos de desigualdad económica y social. Estas experiencias, que le aportan al aprendizaje colectivo, deben enfrentarse con la delicada responsabilidad social que asumen y las implicaciones políticas en juego. De ahí que resulten necesarias nuevas habilidades para el ejercicio de estos procesos que implican la reformulación de la idea del tiempo inherente al proyecto, la construcción de redes y de ámbitos de diálogo nuevos, referidos a la construcción de confianza con las comunidades y a la producción de nuevos protocolos que potencien cadenas de valor agregadas al concepto de construcción colectiva.

El ejercicio de la habilidad técnica, que es una capacidad de cumplimiento de todas las escuelas y que supone que es todo lo necesario para el ejercicio del diseño, no se encuentra habitualmente complementada con el ejercicio de la destreza en la habilidad social que pone en otro plano al diseño como plataforma de producción vincular.

Por habilidad social consideramos la exploración en un plano técnico ligado a formatos de colaboración que no se extinguen en la idea del trabajo grupal que habitualmente llevamos a cabo en los cursos universitarios. El ejercicio de la inteligencia colectiva y de la actitud colaborativa son herramientas necesarias para la construcción de acuerdos y dinámicas de enlace con la comunidad que permitan su inclusión real en el proceso de diseño y construcción. En virtud de ello, también resulta razonable poner en suspenso la naturalización del acto proyectual como fruto de una dinámica autoral, asumiendo lo que significa ir en contra de una tradición que ha consolidado el ejercicio profesional de la arquitectura como una actividad liberal que ha escrito el sentido y la forma de contar la historia a través de la idea de autor.

Quienes encuentran en estas experiencias una oportunidad para el aprendizaje colectivo no suelen establecer procedimientos cerrados ni estructuras fijas. Estos proyectos asumen una condición artesanal que no les permite establecer sistematizaciones. Lo cierto es que cada vínculo social, cada articulación material, cada financiamiento de recursos, necesita una forma específica para ser llevada adelante.

La única materia fija que podría sintetizar una respuesta metodológica para estos procesos es la herramienta de la escucha. Los procesos de conversación, escucha e interpretación operan aquí como una estrategia proyectual y como dispositivo de producción de confianza y afecto. El desarrollo de estos proyectos requiere una etapa inicial de conversación y entrevistas públicas, establecida como un ejercicio de acercamiento al tema y a los problemas a resolver, como también a comprender las proyecciones a futuro y sus limitaciones.

Este ejercicio de pensamiento colectivo que realizamos, consiste en interpretar todo aquello escuchado en las conversaciones con la comunidad, para luego desarrollar un esquema que reúna las necesidades físicas y de infraestructura, la posibilidad de construir en etapas, los posibles crecimientos, las hipótesis de flexibilidad, la transformación de los espacios y la imaginación sobre la máxima dimensión de la obra a realizar.

El interés de involucrar en los procesos de diseño y construcción al usuario y a las personas que lideran las organizaciones sociales o gestionan los espacios que serán activados, tiene por objetivo abrir el trabajo disciplinar de la arquitectura y favorecer el proceso de aprendizaje colectivo. De esta manera potenciamos la construcción de confianza y nos acercamos con mayor precisión a las expectativas creadas. En este ejercicio de acercamiento a la comunidad, normalmente la comunicación toma mayor naturalidad y fluidez con la regularidad y el paso de los días. La escucha hace posible que la dinámica del aprendizaje mutuo a través del intercambio de experiencias, el manejo de herramientas y materiales, y el desafío de las dificultades inevitables, se enriquezca y forme parte importante del acto colaborativo de la construcción.

A menudo, las obras producidas de manera impuesta a la comunidad suelen tener muy poco vínculo afectivo, de apropiación y uso concreto. Esto es muy frecuente en algunas obras públicas construidas con respuestas estandarizadas y sin contacto con quienes serán sus habitantes. Son obras que terminan por caer prematuramente en instancias de degradación y abandono. Por ese motivo es relevante programar momentos específicos de puesta en común del trabajo realizado, donde las personas que integran la comunidad ofrecen críticas, opiniones, preferencias, y en donde todo lo producido es luego pasado por una fase de integración de las ideas que han sido destacadas, trabajando con ellas en un ejercicio colectivo que sintetiza el programa de necesidades y permite avanzar hacia la definición de un proyecto arquitectónico.

Los Talleres de Diseño y Construcción colectiva permiten al estudiante entrar en contacto con los materiales de construcción y transformarlos, verificando sus intenciones dibujadas. Este momento es el resultado de una gran cantidad

de preparativos dirigidos a que cada participante tenga un papel específico, y establezca un grado apreciable de responsabilidad, afecto con el proceso de trabajo y sus resultados. La inclusión de miembros de la comunidad destinataria en los procesos de trabajo constructivo extiende la escucha a todas las fases del proyecto.

Estas experiencias académicas respaldan la necesidad de entender la arquitectura como una disciplina logística, en función de los esfuerzos de la gestión, el desplazamiento de personas y materiales, y la necesaria construcción de acuerdos. Además, recuperan un contenido ancestral relacionado con el acto colectivo de la construcción como hecho de carácter místico e inspirador, que aglutina la fuerza de un vínculo social difícil de obtener mediante otras experiencias humanas.

¿Qué implica posicionar la escucha como una herramienta central en el aprendizaje y en la práctica de la arquitectura? El desarrollo de la capacidad mediadora de la arquitectura solo es posible cuando reconocemos sus vínculos con otros saberes y con la producción colectiva del conocimiento, sin por ello abandonar su lugar en el plano técnico o formal. En ese sentido, la escucha es un acto político porque implica la puesta en marcha de una práctica basada en un vínculo horizontal, en la producción de un diálogo que se transforma en un objeto material a partir de la construcción de un sistema de decisiones. En la disolución de la autoría no se desvanece el valor de la individualidad. Tomando las palabras de Jean Luc Nancy,

la comunidad y la comunicación son constitutivas de la individualidad, más bien que al contrario (y la individualidad no es tal vez, en último término, más que un límite de la comunidad). Pero la comunidad no es tampoco una esencia de todos los individuos, una esencia que estaría dada antes que ellos. Porque la comunidad no es algo distinto de la comunicación de 'seres singulares' separados, que no existen como tales más que a través de la comunicación.[1]

La invitación a ejercitar la arquitectura desde una clave política implica darle mayor protagonismo en el desarrollo de las modalidades de gestión e involucrarnos en las dinámicas sociales de las organizaciones y los grupos humanos con interés en mejorar sus ambientes construidos. Aquí entra en juego la caracterización poblemática de la participación política que Antonio Negri[2] circunscribe en el marco de la crisis de las políticas urbanas, y en las figuras conceptuales del *laboratorio urbano* y del *emprendedor político*.

Por medio de la reproducción de este tipo de talleres y proyectos esperamos que la arquitectura se convierta en una disciplina popular, mediadora de afectos y catalizadora de la identidad de las comunidades. Si bien en la historia de las ciudades latinoamericanas existen ejemplos que lo han logrado y que están presentes en esta antología de casos, la gran deuda histórica reside en la ausencia de popularidad de esta herramienta de cohesión social. La actividad académica en territorios de necesidad y carencia, mediante prácticas de construcción de equipamientos y mejoras del hábitat, implica una nueva matriz intelectual de la disciplina y supone un impacto estético de dimensión política. Conlleva un elevado nivel de compromiso ante las comunidades vulnerables para no defraudar las expectativas creadas. Consiste en asimilar y comprender las condiciones socioambientales.

Ni fenómeno sociológico ni objeto etnográfico: es una visión desde la crisis, una aprehensión de las estructuras de relaciones normadas en medio del colapso perceptivo... Se trata de una inversión del punto de vista: en lugar de profundizar en los análisis sociales sobre la crisis, adoptar el punto de vista de la crisis.[3]

La premisa fundamental de todas estas búsquedas se encuentra apoyada en el entendimiento de la arquitectura como bien social y producto cultural de la comunidad que la genera. Dicho criterio posiciona a la arquitectura como una disciplina que, en función de su capacidad y potencia para la construcción de identidad, favorece la implementación del derecho humano a un hábitat digno en el marco de la satisfacción de las necesidades básicas.

1. Jean Luc Nancy, *La comunidad desobrada* (Madrid: Arena Libros, 2001).
2. Antonio Negri, *De la fábrica a la metrópolis* (Buenos Aires Editorial Cactus, 2020). «Para afrontar positivamente el problema de la participación tal vez sea necesario dar un paso atrás. Es preciso reconsiderar algunas premisas de nuestro discurso. Es en la cooperación social que se generan las condiciones de producción, las dinámicas de valorización, los lazos materiales y la interacción que coordina y orienta la acción humana colectiva que tiene en mira a la producción de bienes y a la reproducción de sus condiciones. Entonces sobre esa base se determina tendencialmente la participación».
3. Diego Sztulwark, *La ofensiva sensible. Neoliberalismo, populismo y el reverso de lo político*, (Buenos Aires: Editorial Caja Negra, 2019).

Ta-
lle-
res

FELIPE MESA
ANA VALDERRAMA
GUSTAVO DIÉGUEZ

TALLER TRAVESÍAS

El Taller de *Travesías por el continente americano* surgió como una serie de reflexiones e intervenciones iniciadas en 1952, luego de la creación del Instituto de Arquitectura de la Pontificia Universidad Católica de Valparaíso por Alberto Cruz y un grupo de artistas y arquitectos diverso: Arturo Baeza, Jaime Bellalta, Fabio Cruz, Miguel Eyquem, Godofredo Iommi, Francisco Méndez, José Vial y Claudio Girola. La primera y mítica travesía realizada en 1965 tuvo el objetivo de materializar un poema épico sobre América del Sur a través de instalaciones efímeras, declamaciones y discusiones con los habitantes del lugar. En esa oportunidad, un grupo de arquitectos, poetas y filósofos partió de Punta Arenas y llegó hasta Santa Cruz de la Sierra, lugar en el que se unen los ejes de la Cruz del Sur. En 1967 publicaron el libro *Amereida* que recogió las experiencias de aquella primera travesía. En 1984 la escuela introdujo las Travesías por América del Sur en su plan de estudios y, desde entonces, los 18 talleres de la escuela viajan una vez por año durante la primavera.

En las travesías, profesores y estudiantes interactúan con comunidades diversas, ponen en juego las relaciones entre arquitectura y palabra poética en un *estar aquí y ahora*. Los proyectos comienzan con la apertura del lugar, a cargo de un poeta que señala el rumbo de la obra. Luego, desarrollan ejercicios para medir y sentir el espacio con el cuerpo y darle forma desde la experiencia. Construyen intervenciones de manera colectiva y abierta, permitiendo ajustes, modificaciones y evoluciones.

La travesía tiene un objetivo triple, viajar, construir y donar. El viaje acerca a los estudiantes a una reflexión sobre el territorio suramericano, haciendo énfasis en todas las tareas necesarias para llevar a cabo la travesía y el proyecto: el viaje, la alimentación, la obra, las finanzas, la salud, el bienestar y el ámbito poético. Profesores y estudiantes se ejercitan en la lectura del territorio a partir de la observación que involucra el dibujo y la anotación. Construyen pequeñas infraestructuras ligadas al lugar, que implican detener el recorrido. Entienden las obras construidas como actos poéticos de carácter efímero al servicio de las comunidades, y como marcas y signos leves en los paisajes, que expresan el acto performativo de aprender haciendo.

TALLER NUBES DE MADERA

Nubes de Madera fue el nombre que un grupo de profesores y estudiantes dieron al conjunto de proyectos que realizaron en el taller de diseño y construcción de la Universidad Pontificia Bolivariana en Medellín, durante los años 2013 y 2017. Este taller vertical para estudiantes de tercer y cuarto año, llevó a cabo la construcción de diez edificios de pequeño formato en zonas rurales del departamento de Antioquia, uno cada semestre. En asocio con los municipios rurales de San Vicente Ferrer y Támesis, y con apoyo técnico de la empresa local de construcción en madera inmunizada Serye, el curso construyó edificios culturales y educativos para comunidades vulnerables.

Cada semestre, un equipo liderado por dos profesores —Miguel Mesa y Felipe Mesa— y 30 estudiantes, gestionó recursos económicos por medio de rifas y donaciones. Construyó una relación con líderes municipales identificando necesidades de comunidades rurales. Los estudiantes diseñaron varias opciones arquitectónicas y desarrollaron la más interesante de manera colaborativa y con tareas específicas. Llevaron a cabo presupuestos de obra y construyeron pequeños edificios de madera con apoyo de ingenieros, constructores y líderes sociales. Entregaron edificios a las comunidades, intercambiando tiempo y conocimiento. Dieron vida a un grupo de edificios livianos, permeables y bioclimáticos, además de resistentes, económicos y de bajo mantenimiento usando madera inmunizada como principal material de construcción —madera de pino Pátula, cultivada, certificada y sostenible—. Exploraron un sistema estructural de columnas, vigas y riostras diagonales, articuladas por medio de pernos de acero galvanizado.

Este curso entendió la idea de complejidad en arquitectura como el proceso necesario para construir un edificio de manera colaborativa, con todas sus etapas y actores involucrados. Para sus profesores, los edificios construidos poseen formas posibles y necesarias, y son también expresión de las restricciones en juego. El curso hizo más énfasis en el trabajo colaborativo entre estudiantes que en el trabajo individual, y dio mayor importancia a la construcción que a la representación en dibujos y maquetas. En palabras de Miguel Mesa y Felipe Mesa, «así como un estudiante de medicina debe aprender a tratar un paciente en un hospital, un estudiante de arquitectura debe aprender a diseñar, construir e interactuar con comunidades y clientes en lugares concretos». Según ellos, resulta importante que los estudiantes encuentren un balance entre la representación arquitectónica, el diseño y la construcción durante su carrera.

TALLER AL BORDE

Taller Al Borde es el nombre que la oficina ecuatoriana de arquitectura del mismo nombre ha dado a sus participaciones académicas en algunas universidades de Ecuador, Perú y Chile, bajo diversos formatos y modalidades. Durante los años 2015, 2016 y 2017, este grupo dirigió un taller de diseño y construcción en la Universidad Tecnológica Indoamérica, UTI, localizada en Ambato, a dos horas de Quito. Este taller, para estudiantes de cuarto año de carrera, construyó durante dos años y medio más de 50 edificios o intervenciones de pequeño formato en zonas periféricas de Ambato y zonas rurales cercanas.

Cada versión del curso recibió 25 estudiantes que trabajaron de manera individual o en grupos pequeños, planteando problemas de diseño arquitectónico en relación con su vida cotidiana. Para responder al tema definido, gestionaron recursos económicos y materiales, involucraron familiares o personas cercanas, eligieron lugares, programas, construyeron y usaron los nuevos espacios, todo en un tiempo récord de cuatro meses y medio. Cada proyecto implicó la aplicación de estrategias cambiantes, el uso de materiales heterogéneos —guadua, madera, metal, concreto, ladrillos, vidrio, paja, etc.—, tecnologías locales y la generación de programas livianos —miradores, habitaciones, espacios para meditar, espacios para lectura, entre otros —. En algunos casos los estudiantes siguen hoy usando estas construcciones, situación que les permite tener una experiencia de primera mano, hacer mantenimiento, reformas o ampliaciones.

En sus Talleres de diseño y construcción de la UTI, Al Borde hizo énfasis en el trabajo fuera de los salones de clase, intentando borrar la diferencia entre academia y práctica profesional. Propusieron a sus estudiantes salir de su zona de confort, sacando lo mejor de situaciones restringidas para dar vida los nuevos proyectos. Invitaron a los participantes a enfrentar la realidad cotidiana, entendiendo el proyecto arquitectónico como un desafío positivo. Finalmente, participaron como facilitadores entre los estudiantes y la comunidad, estimulando el trabajo con la gente y el conocimiento extraído de las prácticas habituales.

TALLER ACTIVO

Activo es el nombre del taller de Diseño y Construcción de la Facultad de Arquitectura del Instituto Tecnológico y de Estudios Superiores de Monterrey, Sede Querétaro, dirigido por el profesor Alfonso Garduño entre los años 2012 y 2015. Este curso recibió inicialmente estudiantes de tercer año y, posteriormente, acogió a estudiantes de quinto año con mayor experiencia. Durante este periodo el taller llevó a cabo la construcción de más de diez proyectos de pequeño formato en asocio con diversas comunidades de vecinos de las periferias urbanas de Querétaro. Su nombre expresa el interés por una arquitectura participativa, con impactos concretos y positivos para estudiantes y comunidades.

Cada cuatrimestre académico el curso recibió entre doce y quince estudiantes que trabajaron en equipos de tres y cuatro participantes. Durante el primer mes realizaron investigaciones de campo y, asesorados por la profesora Estefanía Bondi, entraron en contacto con líderes comunitarios. Además, gestionaron recursos económicos y materiales por medio de fiestas, rifas, donaciones privadas y apoyo de la universidad. En el segundo mes, diseñaron y presentaron opciones de proyectos a la comunidad y a un jurado amplio, que eligió la propuesta más pertinente. A partir de ese momento y durante el tercer mes, estudiantes y profesores trabajaron juntos desarrollando la propuesta elegida. En el cuarto mes construyeron el proyecto con ayuda de empresas, obreros calificados y mano de obra de la comunidad.

Este curso trabajó con el interés de que los procesos participativos, que muchas veces se quedan en buenas intenciones, condujeran a la construcción de proyectos concretos, ligados a los recursos disponibles. Siempre intentaron ofrecer a las comunidades algo más de lo que esperaban del proyecto, con programas abiertos, flexibles, cualidades espaciales, tectónicas y materiales sencillos pero resistentes y con bajo mantenimiento. A medida que el curso construyó edificios de pequeño formato en la misma zona de la periferia urbana de Querétaro, el equipo de trabajo planeó estas intervenciones como *acupuntura* urbana, con un impacto a mayor escala en el tejido social y el potencial de transformar el territorio.

TALLER A77

El Taller a77 es un equipo de arquitectura liderado por Gustavo Diéguez y Lucas Gilardi que desarrolla diversas modalidades y formatos para la producción de talleres de diseño y construcción colectiva, con la participación de estudiantes en la fabricación de equipamientos comunitarios. Inicialmente tuvieron experiencias con proyectos autogestionados por fuera de los espacios académicos y a través de convocatorias abiertas para la participación multidisciplinaria de estudiantes. En segunda instancia, realizaron proyectos encargados por dependencias estatales con recursos públicos. En la actualidad alternan proyectos convocados por organizaciones civiles, y proyectos que lideran como profesores en los talleres de diseño y construcción de dos universidades públicas.

En todos los casos, Taller a77 hace énfasis en un diálogo fluido con la comunidad a través de diversas dinámicas sociales —ejercicios de escucha y formulación de acuerdos— que permiten elaborar un conocimiento colectivo acerca de aquello que será construido, planteando programas, etapas y técnicas disponibles.

En los casos organizados desde los cursos universitarios, las propuestas de los estudiantes emergen a partir de un diálogo continuo con las organizaciones sociales y tienen instancias de presentación pública a la comunidad. En algunas ocasiones los equipos de trabajo eligen un solo diseño que luego desarrollan constructivamente y, en otras, integran las mejores ideas de diseño, produciendo una versión final.

Los integrantes de a77 dan gran importancia al diseño de una logística en la que todos los participantes entrelazan sus funciones. En sus talleres de construcción colectiva, por lo general realizados durante las vacaciones, favorecen la construcción de piezas prefabricadas en taller, que luego ensamblan, reduciendo los tiempos de construcción. Las jornadas de trabajo, tanto en el taller como en el sitio, permiten que los estudiantes aprendan destrezas manuales, el uso de herramientas y el ingenio necesario para sistematizar la construcción y las tareas de una obra.

TALLER LAB.PRO.FAB

Taller Lab.Pro.Fab es el nombre que el arquitecto y profesor venezolano Alejandro Haiek da a sus talleres de diseño y fabricación en diversas universidades latinoamericanas e internacionales. Lab.Pro.Fab es también el nombre de su laboratorio de proyectos, dedicado a la hibridación de tecnologías tradicionales y novedosas, y a la reflexión ecosocial contemporánea. Durante el año 2010, Alejandro lideró un taller de diseño y construcción en la Universidad Simón Bolívar en Caracas. Este curso para estudiantes de tercer año, enfocado en darle una segunda vida a materiales donados y en desuso, construyó nuevos espacios y prototipos, buscando el bienestar de la comunidad universitaria en la ciudad de Caracas.

El Taller recibió 18 estudiantes que trabajaron de manera colaborativa durante cuatro meses, estudiando los componentes básicos de la arquitectura: estructura, piso, pare[d]y [te]cho. El equipo de trabajo, asesorado p[or los] talleres de construcción de la univer[sidad,] gestionó recursos, evaluó técnicas con[struc]tivas, y construyó componentes modular[es que] luego articuló en un nuevo espacio abier[to a la] comunidad académica.

Los Talleres Lab.Pro.Fab hacen énfasi[s en la] dimensión técnica y el potencial artíst[ico de] la arquitectura, fomentando en los est[udian]tes la experimentación material y la ref[lexión] formal, de esta manera favorecen tamb[ién la] responsabilidad social de la disciplina. [Estos] cursos apuestan por una arquitectura inm[ediata] y de calidad, acercando a los estudiantes [a las] estéticas emergentes del reciclaje, el r[euso y] la hibridación.

TALLER PEI

El Taller PEI es el Programa de Estudi[os In]ternacionales de la Facultad de Arquite[ctura y] Diseño de la Pontificia Universidad Jav[eriana] en Bogotá, dirigido por el profesor Carlo[s Her]nández. Este curso fundado en 1996, tie[ne vo]cación interdisciplinaria y funciona por [medio] de talleres intensos de diseño, dirigid[os por] un grupo de profesores de planta, y prof[esores] invitados nacionales e internacionales, [que van] cambiando según las temáticas. El PEI rec[ibe en] promedio 80 estudiantes de arquitectura y [dise]ño por semestre, que trabajan de manera c[olabo]rativa frente a temáticas diversas, expl[orando] siempre territorios novedosos en los camp[os del] arte, la arquitectura, la filosofía, las [nuevas] tecnologías y la ecología.

Durante los años 2010, 2011 y 2012, [el PEI] trabajó en alianza con comunidades del [muni]cipio de Palomino, en el departamento [de La] Guajira. Por medio de varios cursos acadé[micos,] visitas y talleres, que involucraron la [parti]cipación de los colectivos españoles Zul[oark y] Zoohaus, y a la plataforma abierta de inv[esti]gación y diseño Inteligencias Colectiva[s, el] Programa de Estudios Internacionales prop[uso un] plan maestro de actuación, y lo impleme[ntó por] medio de proyectos arquitectónicos de d[iversa] índole y escala.

Palomino, Sociedad en Construcción, [es el] nombre de esta intervención, en la que u[n gru]po de profesores, estudiantes, líderes [comu]nitarios y asesores, gestionaron, dise[ñaron] y construyeron una diversidad de proyect[os con] cualidades sostenibles, haciendo uso d[e téc]nicas y materiales locales de bajo cost[o. Con] apoyo económico diverso —institucional, [de los] profesores y los estudiantes— el equipo d[e tra]bajo viajó más de seis veces, se instal[ó en el] lugar, y se integró a la comunidad por periodos de tiempo variables que permitieron la construcción de una red de infraestructuras comunitarias y privadas de pequeño formato, enfocadas en la higiene, la recolección de agua lluvia, la seguridad alimentaria y en torno a actividades culturales y de esparcimiento: una nueva casa de la cultura, una casa de los deportes, tribunas para la cancha de fútbol, amoblamiento urbano, pozos de agua y baños secos, entre otros.

El Taller PEI cree en una educación de la arquitectura interdisciplinaria, internacional, colaborativa y abierta. Mezclando estudiantes de tercero y cuarto año, hace mayor énfasis en temas contemporáneos relevantes —nuevos medios digitales, y fenómenos ecosociales—, que en aspectos disciplinares y tradicionales del campo de la arquitectura. Su intervención en Palomino propone un modelo pedagógico participativo y de largo aliento, que implicó vivir, construir y habitar con las comunidades vulnerables en sus territorios.

TALLER MATÉRICOS PERIFÉRICOS

Matéricos Periféricos es un colectivo destinado a contribuir a la justicia socio-espacial de las ciudades latinoamericanas. Está constituido por 40 docentes de la Facultad de Arquitectura de Rosario, graduados y estudiantes que anualmente se ofrecen como voluntarios en talleres de proyecto y construcción. Desde 1997, Matéricos Periféricos se posicionó en la centralidad de las periferias, estudiando sus patrones sociales y físicos por medio de proyectos de investigación que arrojaron mapas, diagramas y especulaciones. En el año 2001, con la gran crisis de Argentina, el grupo decidió avanzar en acciones directas en el territorio a partir de la coconstrucción de equipamientos comunitarios realizados a través de talleres de diseño y construcción. Desde ese entonces, dichos talleres forman parte del plan de trabajo de los cursos verticales Barrale y Valderrama, y de dos asignaturas optativas. Los talleres se desarrollan en dos modalidades: un taller concentrado en dos meses, de octubre a diciembre; y un taller expandido, que consta de jornadas de trabajo distribuidas durante todo el año. Dependiendo de cada proyecto, los estudiantes participan de todo o parte del proceso de coconstrucción.

Las obras de Matéricos Periféricos tienen objetivos diversos, entre ellos, apuntalar a las instituciones locales en sus actividades comunitarias, desafiar la agencia estatal, devolver tierras públicas a la comunidad, producir marcas en los paisajes o activar pequeñas cooperativas. Durante los talleres de diseño y construcción, los participantes —estudiantes, docentes y la comunidad— cogestionan y coproducen artefactos y equipamientos comunitarios que se conciben como dispositivos capaces de catalizar y manifestar —en su proceso de producción, espacio y forma— procesos periféricos, materiales, tradiciones artesanales y dinámicas sociales. Con el tiempo, algunos de los artefactos han provocado mejoras infraestructurales adicionales: su presencia física ha obligado a intervenciones públicas que de otro modo no hubieran ocurrido.

TALLER DE TITULACIÓN DE TALCA

La Escuela de Arquitectura de la Universidad de Talca se fundó en 1998 cuando el Consejo de Rectores aprobó el proyecto académico elaborado por el arquitecto Juan Román. En el año 2001 se definió el currículum académico que persiste hasta la fecha con una organización en bimestres. El plan de estudios de la escuela se fundamenta en tres pilares: una mirada situada en el Valle Central de Chile como territorio de reflexión y acción, el foco en la cultura material, y un aprender haciendo por medio de talleres de diseño y construcción. Se realizan cuatro tipos de talleres consecutivos y acumulativos: primero, el Taller de la Materia para los estudiantes de primer año —en el que destaca el ejercicio del cubo de materia—; segundo, el Taller del Cuerpo, también para primer año, se ocupa de reconocerse en el espacio y configurar las dinámicas del movimiento. Tercero, el Taller de Agosto o Taller de Obra, en el que participan los estudiantes de la escuela construyendo proyectos a pequeña escala en el Valle Central de Chile. Y, por último, el Taller de Titulación, que realizan los estudiantes del último año quienes deben integrar componentes de investigación, gestión, proyecto, construcción y difusión de la obra.

En 2004 se realizó el primer Taller de Titulación, que es la manifestación más significativa de la producción de la Escuela y del perfil del egresado. El estudiante culmina con el proyecto y la construcción de una obra in situ. El Taller de Titulación es individual y requiere que el estudiante defina las condiciones previas, se involucre con las comunidades, construya una red de relaciones que le permita movilizar las energías para que la obra ocurra, al tiempo que gestione y ejecute las posibilidades materiales, financieras y de construcción de la obra. El taller tiene una duración de ocho meses y comienza en marzo con la definición del lugar, el problema o tema de investigación. En mayo y junio el estudiante elabora la idea general y el proyecto. En julio y agosto realiza los detalles constructivos y expone el proyecto ante un grupo evaluador para optar al pase de construcción. Durante los dos meses siguientes realiza la construcción de la obra. Desde la implementación de este programa, la escuela ha construido más de 700 proyectos en distintos puntos Valle Central de Chile, que han servido para afianzar los lazos comunitarios de la región.

TALLER PAAF

El Programa Académico de Asistencia Federal, PAAF, está incorporado a la estructura de la carrera de arquitectura de la Universidad de Morón dentro de la materia Proyecto Final Integrador, en la que los estudiantes gestionan, diseñan y construyen proyectos para destinatarios específicos. Este programa constituye una política de extensión universitaria que promueve la construcción de infraestructuras comunitarias de pequeño formato para comunidades vulnerables. Inicialmente los estudiantes entraban en contacto con las comunidades, detectaban necesidades y proponían los proyectos a construir. Más adelante, y de manera sistemática, la universidad realizó acuerdos con organizaciones civiles, definiendo proyectos con mayor estabilidad e impacto. Por ejemplo, el convenio con el municipio del Tigre, en el norte de la Provincia de Buenos Aires, permitió a cien estudiantes desarrollar diversos proyectos en un barrio vulnerable. En esa ocasión, construyeron nueve casas, un vivero y gestionaron mejoras en el espacio público.

Actualmente, cuatro profesores lideran el curso haciendo énfasis en los siguientes temas: gestión, tecnología, estructura, diseño, supervisión de obra, urbanismo y paisajismo. Por lo general, las intervenciones son de pequeño formato, pero en algunos casos configuran estrategias territoriales. El programa gestiona recursos económicos por medio de congresos y conferencias de arquitectura, y gestiona donaciones de materiales realizadas por empresas privadas y municipios. En muchos casos las instituciones atendidas aportan mano de obra, y los estudiantes aportan recursos económicos que de cualquier modo invertirían en cursos convencionales de diseño. El taller PAAF apoya la autonomía de sus estudiantes y los alienta a responder a sus preocupaciones disciplinares y sociales por medio de sus proyectos construidos. Hace énfasis en una arquitectura solidaria y sostenible.

TALLER DE INTERVENCIÓN COMUNITARIA

El Taller de Intervención Comunitaria es un curso de Titulación de la Facultad de Arquitectura de la Universidad de las Américas en Santiago de Chile, inscrito en un programa multidisciplinar de intervenciones comunitarias desarrollado por la universidad. En esta modalidad el curso interactúa con barrios de la ciudad, proponiendo intervenciones ligadas a las necesidades de sus habitantes. Para ello recibe un grupo pequeño de estudiantes —entre 10 y 12 participantes— que trabaja de manera colaborativa e individual durante un año y medio con profesores, asesores de otras escuelas y organizaciones de vecinos. Durante los años 2021 y 2022, un grupo de estudiantes trabajó en la villa Músicos del Mundo proponiendo como evento final un Festival de arquitectura en el barrio, con seis intervenciones arquitectónicas de pequeña escala, mezclando actividades lúdicas, arte urbano y performances celebrativas. Esta última versión del Taller de Titulación que los profesores nombraron *Travesías en La Incertidumbre*, fue desarrollada en tres cuatrimestres académicos. En el primero, los estudiantes en grupo hicieron un diagnóstico y cogestionaron la intervención con la comunidad, consiguieron apoyos económicos y acordaron los programas; en el segundo, codiseñaron los proyectos en el barrio de manera individual y, en el tercero, coimplementaron o construyeron los nuevos espacios. La universidad apoyó estas intervenciones con recursos económicos —máximo un tercio del valor total de cada proyecto— y los estudiantes gestionaron recursos por medio de rifas y donaciones.

Este taller, que sigue hoy en funcionamiento, entiende la academia como práctica social crítica, y el proyecto construido, como un instrumento mediador entre los procesos pedagógicos y los fenómenos socio-ambientales que ocurren en los barrios de Santiago de Chile. Asume el diseño arquitectónico como un proceso multidisciplinario y colaborativo, dirigido a la construcción de bienes comunes. Favorece programas sociales que van más allá de las necesidades inmediatas de las comunidades, apuntando a la reflexión y a lo inesperado.

TALLER DANZA

El Taller Danza es una de las nueve cátedras de proyecto arquitectónico de la FADU-UdelaR, que tiene cursos en todos los años de la carrera de Arquitectura. Durante el primer año este taller lleva a cabo experiencias de construcción colectiva. Los ejercicios son, por lo general, intervenciones en el espacio público definidas previamente por los profesores en colaboración con autoridades municipales. Las intervenciones, realizadas en equipo por profesores y estudiantes, pretenden intensificar el uso de espacios públicos subutilizados a través de arquitecturas efímeras durante periodos de tiempo que van entre uno y tres meses. Para gestionar económicamente los proyectos, los participantes conforman una cooperativa aportando cada uno el costo de lo que normalmente invertirían en un taller de diseño convencional. En algunos casos reciben también donaciones y aportes diversos.

En cada versión del curso, los profesores distribuyen el trabajo en cinco equipos de veinte estudiantes aproximadamente. Cada grupo desarrolla varios proyectos durante tres semanas y escoge el más interesante. Luego un jurado externo elige el proyecto que será construido entre las propuestas de cada grupo. El proyecto elegido pasa a ser de todos, y a partir de allí los equipos se organizan en comisiones por temas de interés: prototipos, detalles constructivos, iluminación, difusión y logística. Luego de un mes de trabajo en el desarrollo del proyecto, los participantes, dirigidos por el equipo de prototipos, construyen el proyecto de manera colaborativa en una semana y lo inauguran con las comunidades.

Los profesores del taller de diseño y construcción del Taller Danza, hacen énfasis en arquitecturas transitorias y livianas, con la capacidad de detonar nuevos usos y programas en el espacio público consolidado de la ciudad, muchas veces en desuso o abandonado. Entienden la arquitectura como un acontecimiento público o como un evento colectivo. Por medio de geometrías modulares y cambiantes, los estudiantes proponen intervenciones que dinamizan la ciudad y favorecen la reapropiación de los espacios públicos por parte de los ciudadanos.

TALLER E

El Taller E surgió por la iniciativa de cuatro profesores, Juanchi Giangreco, Lucho Elgue, Javier Corvalán y Solano Benítez, que buscaban maneras alternativas de enseñanza. Este curso vertical fue planeado como una cátedra a lo largo de toda la carrera, haciendo énfasis en diversos aspectos del proyecto arquitectónico en cada semestre. Durante los años 2018, 2019 y 2020, con un grupo de 30 estudiantes en cada curso, los profesores Lukas Fuster, Sergio Ybarra y Guido Yambay, lideraron el tercer semestre de la cátedra, dando importancia al estudio de las estructuras en arquitectura y

sus cualidades tectónicas y formales. Inicialmente, construyeron maquetas de gran formato en hormigón, madera y espaguetis que fueron sometidas a pruebas de carga. Posteriormente, gestionaron recursos y materiales para construir edificios de pequeño formato al servicio de la comunidad universitaria.

Cada semestre los estudiantes trabajaron en diez grupos, gestionando recursos, definiendo programas pertinentes y diseñando proyectos con diferentes materiales y cualidades estructurales. Luego de evaluar diversas opciones, eligieron la mejor propuesta para desarrollarla de manera colaborativa, con diferentes funciones: presupuesto, compras, detalles, construcción, etc. Las construcciones llevadas a cabo de manera intensa y durante tres semanas, son el resultado sutil entre la abstracción requerida para entender las implicaciones estructurales y constructivas en juego, y el interés por ligar el proyecto con el contexto universitario del campus y la ciudad.

Este curso hizo énfasis no solo en el diseño arquitectónico, sino también en la importancia de entender los proyectos como fenómenos técnicos, sostenibles y de gestión. Por lo tanto, el contacto con donantes, usuarios y con las herramientas de construcción y materiales, fue determinante en el proceso académico seguido por estudiantes y profesores.

ATARRAYA TALLER

Atarraya Taller es el nombre del taller de investigación-acción de los arquitectos y profesores ecuatorianos Lorena Burbano y Sebastián Oviedo, diseñado para colaborar con organizaciones sociales, entidades públicas e instituciones educativas, con el interés de gestionar procesos participativos de producción del hábitat, en conjunto con comunidades, colectivos y movimientos de Latinoamérica. Entre 2017 y 2018, trabajaron con la organización chamangueña Opción Más, la Universidad Estatal de Portland, la Universidad de Tokio y la Universidad de Ciencias Aplicadas de Múnich para gestionar, diseñar y construir con estudiantes anga, un pueblo pesquero gravemente afectado por el terremoto que sufrió Ecuador en 2016. Durante los años 2018 y 2019 trabajaron como docentes en la Universidad de Ciencias aplicadas de Múnich —bajo la dirección de la profesora Ursula Hartig— para gestionar, diseñar y construir con estudiantes un centro de cultura y ecología en asocio con la comunidad de Santa Catarina Quiané, en Oaxaca, México.

Cada uno de estos proyectos recibió un promedio de 20 estudiantes que trabajó en equipo con profesores, asesores y líderes comunitarios para gestionar recursos, diseñar los centros culturales y construirlos en dos fases. En el primer caso, estudiantes estadounidenses, japoneses y alemanes, viajaron con profesores a Ecuador; y en el segundo, estudiantes alemanes y profesores se desplazaron a México, en donde se sumaron a estudiantes locales. En ambas ocasiones convivieron con las comunidades durante el tiempo de la construcción, mezclando técnicas locales, materiales disponibles y conocimientos disciplinares. Los nuevos edificios poseen geometrías y espacialidades sencillas, acogedoras y permeables.

El nombre *Atarraya* hace referencia a la cultura pesquera, y es una metáfora del tejido de relaciones que constituye las intervenciones sociales y espaciales. En sus cursos y proyectos, Atarraya Taller se mueve a lo largo de todas las actividades proyectuales gestionando, diseñando y construyendo. Trabaja con organizaciones cuyo horizonte político se articula desde las contribuciones de diferentes saberes y acciones, intentando desacralizar el conocimiento académico como única verdad.

Design-Build Studios in Latin America
was printed in March 2023.